A Guide to the Common Core Writing Workshop

Primary Grades

Lucy Calkins

Photography by Peter Cunningham

HEINEMANN ◆ PORTSMOUTH, NH

Heinemann
361 Hanover Street
Portsmouth, NH 03801–3912
www.heinemann.com

Offices and agents throughout the world

ISBN-13: 978-0-325-04798-0

Production: Elizabeth Valway, David Stirling, and Abigail Heim
Cover and interior designs: Jenny Jensen Greenleaf
Series includes photography by Peter Cunningham, Nadine Baldasare, and Elizabeth Dunford
Composition: Publishers' Design and Production Services, Inc.
Manufacturing: Steve Bernier

Printed in the United States of America on acid-free paper

20 19 18 17 16 VP 10 9 8 7 6

Contents

Acknowledgments

THIS SERIES is the biggest undertaking of my life—other than the larger projects of leading the Teachers College Reading and Writing Project and of parenting Miles and Evan—and so it is fitting that I dedicate this project to my mother and my father. I thank Evan and Virginia Calkins for all that I am, for all that I believe in, and for giving me eight brothers and sisters—Sally, Steve, Joan, Ben, Hugh, Ellen, Geoff, and Tim—and thirty-some nieces and nephews. Two of the many young people in the extended clan are my sons, Miles and Evan Skorpen. Anyone who has ever read my writing or been part of my teaching knows that the sun rises and sets for me with Miles and Evan. Those of you who have followed their writing through all the years may miss the new infusions of their drafts; they both have become young men now, and I'm not chronicling their comings and goings in quite the same way. John and I could not be more proud of them.

I live and learn as part of the community of teacher-educators that comprises the Teachers College Reading and Writing Project, and all of the people at the project are my thought-companions. I especially thank Laurie Pessah and Kathleen Tolan, senior deputy directors; Mary Ehrenworth, deputy director for middle school and coauthor of *Pathways to the Common Core*; and Amanda Hartman, associate director. These people are my closest friends, my life partners, and I can't imagine any more beautiful way to work and live than alongside them. I also thank Mary Ann Mustac and the team of fifty-plus full-time staff developers who keep the project's work vital, robust, and grounded. These people, too, are my partners.

At the desk, my closest partner is Kate Montgomery. Kate and I have imagined, planned, written, and revised all the Units of Study series, since their origin. I was only willing to undertake this gigantic, all-new CCSS–aligned effort after Kate agreed to work half-time as essentially the senior coauthor of the entire series. Kate's brilliant mind is ever-present in all of these books and in the design of the entire effort.

The ideas about teaching writing that are essential in this book have been evolving since I was a young teacher. Starting then and continuing for years afterward, I worked very closely with two people who opened the field of writing to me and to the world. Other than my parents, Don Graves and Don Murray changed my life more than anyone else. My pathway would have been entirely different had these two incredible mentors not shown me a terrain to explore; they gave me tools with which to do that exploring, and most of all, they empowered me to rise to the occasion.

Words can't easily contain my gratitude to all the coauthors who joined me in writing these books. I thank each individually within the particular books, but some have helped with books beyond their own. Amanda Hartman's knowledge of young children has been like a bottomless well from which many of us drink continually. Julia Mooney's impeccable standards and her deep knowledge make her a pillar of strength. Kathleen Tolan's originality and her fearless focus on excellence make her a never-ending source of insight. In a ten-minute conversation, Mary Ehrenworth can illuminate any conundrum, helping me see a path. She has also helped me care deeply about the Common Core State Standards. Ali Marron's writing skill and enormous heart have made her the perfect person to have close by during writing work. Kelly Boland Hohne's searing intelligence has left many of us feeling breathless—and blessed. Janet Steinberg's hand on the pulse of teacher effectiveness, curricular mapping, Depth of Knowledge (DOK), and the CCSS has kept us all hopping. Audra Robb has made us smarter in the arena of performance assessments. The infusion of fresh potent teaching from Hareem Khan, often working by candlelight due to power failures in remote corners of

Pakistan, has kept us going. Many school principals have opened their doors to us—none more often than Adele Schroder, PS 59; Melanie Woods, PS 29; Anthony Inzerillo, 199 Queens; Katy Rosen, 199 Manhattan; Daryl Adalhoff, PS 158; and Cheryl Tyler 277, Bronx. Peter Cunningham, the photographer for every book I've ever written, graced this effort with magical talent.

Teva Blair and Abby Heim worked together with Kate Montgomery to lead Heinemann's involvement with this effort, and I thank them both for channeling enormous support toward this project. Teva Blair has kept her hand on the pulse of the entire enterprise, managing the people, the texts, and the dates and, above all, bringing a knack for structure and knowledge of the project to her marvelous editing efforts. Abby Heim has been the production mastermind at Heinemann. She has kept track of all the zillions of bits and pieces that create the mosaic of these books, and has done so with a combination of strength, resolve, and focus that keeps everyone's attention on the job at hand. She's also been the emotional leader of the enterprise, bringing maturity and experience to that role. This team works under the direction of Lesa Scott, who is at the helm of Heinemann, and I thank her for recognizing the significance of this effort and devoting resources and talent to it. Charles McQuillen and Buzz Rhodes will take over once Abby and Teva let go, and I thank them in advance for what they will do to usher the books into the hands of teachers.

Most of all, I am grateful to Kate Montgomery, who is my writing partner and the co-leader of this entire effort. Kate and I imagined the series together, made the hard decisions together, devised the principles and structures that unify the series together, and supported the coauthors together. It has been a great joy to share responsibility for authoring the ideas and the books in the series with Kate. Her writing embodies the crystal clarity and the warmth that E. B. White describes in his *Elements of Style*. Her knowledge of teaching and literacy research has grown from a lifetime of work with many of the best thinkers in the field. How blessed this project has been to have her constant and close involvement.

A Note to My Readers

IN A MOMENT, I'm going to ask that you step with me into this series, into this world of writing plans and teaching strategies and exciting new ideas for fostering developmental breakthroughs in children. In some ways I think of this project as the culmination of my life work so far; it grows from decades of think tanks and teaching and coaching and studying with my colleagues and with teachers from around the world. It represents not only my best work, but also the best work of more than thirty of my colleagues. This is the grand unveiling of this master work, and I am so eager to share it with you!

Nonetheless, I want to ask you to stop for a moment, before you read on. Before you turn to the ins and outs of curriculum and the face of education today and new standards and old standards and best practices, pause for a moment to picture the face of a child. One small someone you know well. When you see her running up to you, does it make you smile? When you picture him, walking slowly away with his head down, backpack slumped over his shoulder, do you want to reach out, maybe call him back? And when you think of all of them, their quirky, tousled, grubby, beautiful faces looking up at you expectantly, I know you feel the tug in your chest, that tug of feeling that we are so responsible for them all. We feel it deeply. And this is what I want to say: that is the core of all that matters in teaching. Without that care, the greatest curriculum in the world is only paper and a little dry ink.

Chapter 1

A New Mission for Schools and Educators

The new mission . . . is to get all students to meet high standards of education and to provide them with a lifelong education that does not have built-in obsolescence of so much old-style curriculum but that equips them to be lifelong learners.

—Michael Fullan, Peter Hill, and Carmel Crevola from *Breakthrough* (2006)

I N A WORLD that is increasingly dominated by big corporations and big money, it is easy for individuals to feel silenced. No one is more apt to be silenced than children, who too often grow up being taught to be obedient more than to be wise, empathetic, and critical. The teaching of writing can change that. In a democracy, we must help young people grow up to know how to voice their ideas, to speak out for what is right and good.

The information age of today makes it especially imperative that young people, not just an elite few, but all students, develop skills that are significantly higher than those that have been required of them in the past. In part, the increased focus on writing comes from the technological revolution that has transformed our lives. As the ways of communicating seep into every nook and cranny of our day—text messaging, email, social media, search engines—all of us are using writing more than ever. Today, it has become increasingly important that all children are given an education that enables them to synthesize, organize, reflect on, and respond to the data in their world. Indeed, several years ago, the National Commission on Writing called for a "writing revolution," suggesting that children need to double the amount of time they spend writing in their classrooms. Students need to be able not only to write narratives, but also to write arguments and information texts. They need not only to record information and ideas, but to synthesize, analyze, compare, and contrast that information and those ideas.

In their important book, *Breakthrough* (2006), Michael Fullan, Peter Hill, and Carmel Crevola point out that the old mission for schools used to be to provide universal access to basic education and then to provide a small elite with access to university education. Although that mission may have made sense in the world of our parents, it doesn't make sense any longer. Whereas twenty years ago 95% of jobs were low-skilled, today those jobs only constitute 10% of our entire economy (Darling-Hammond et al. *Powerful Learning: What We Know about Teaching for Understanding*, 2008). Children who leave school today without strong literacy skills will no longer find a job waiting for them. "The new mission . . . is to get *all* students to meet high standards of education and to provide them with a lifelong education that does not have built-in obsolescence of so much old-style curriculum but that equips them to be lifelong learners." These words are from the prelude to *Breakthrough*, but they could also be in the opening page of this book.

As this nation wakes up to the fact that the education millions of Americans received in the past simply isn't adequate for today, more and more schools are realizing that one of the most potent ways to accelerate students' progress as learners is by equipping them with first-rate skills in writing. While the teaching of writing had no place in the No Child Left Behind (NCLB) standards of yesteryear, there has been an about-face since then, and the Common Core State Standards give equal attention to writing as to reading—and even suggest that students' abilities to read will be assessed through their abilities to write.

For teachers, parents, and students in schools that have not taught writing in the past, the exemplar student writing that is showcased in Appendix B of the Common Core (describing the standards themselves, which detail what all students are expected to know and be able to do) feel like pie in the sky. I've seen teachers guffaw at some of the samples of writing that are included in the Common Core as if that work represents an utterly inaccessible goal. That's not a surprising response from educators who have not, themselves, received help teaching writing.

What we now know about writing development is that students need extensive opportunities to write on topics they care about, they need explicit and sequenced instruction that helps them progress along a learning continuum, and they need critical feedback that helps them know next steps. It's a tall order for teachers to provide those conditions to students when teachers, themselves, have generally received almost no instruction at all in writing.

But the good news is that the student samples in the Appendix B are representative of what many students have been doing for a long time. Educators need not feel empty-handed when they ask, "How can we begin to approach Common Core expectations in writing?" Instead, there are schools across the country that have traveled at least a good portion of that journey and can help other schools get started. That is, although many school leaders are just now waking up to the importance of teaching writing, many of us across the nation have had those concerns at heart for a long time. At the Teachers College Reading and Writing Project, for example, we have been working for three decades to develop, pilot, revise, and implement state-of-the-art curriculum in writing. We have had a chance to do this work under the influence of the Common Core for the past few years, and this series—this treasure chest of experiences, theories, techniques, tried-and-true methods, and questions—will bring the results of that work to you.

THE WRITING WORKSHOP: GROWTH FOR STUDENTS *AND* TEACHERS

Word has spread. The hundreds of thousands of teachers who used an earlier, very different edition of this series have spread the word that the writing workshop has given their children unbelievable power not only as writers, but also as thinkers, learners, and readers. School districts are finding that when teachers receive the education they deserve in the teaching of writing, those teachers are able to provide students with clear, sequenced, vibrant instruction in writing (along with opportunities to write daily for their own important purposes), and this makes a dramatic difference in young people's abilities to write. Powerful writing instruction produces visible and immediate results; the stories, petitions, speeches, and essays that students produce become far more substantial and significant, revealing the young authors' ideas in ways that make parents, community members, and the children themselves sit up and take notice.

When young people are explicitly taught the craft of proficient writing, they are able to travel the world as writers, applying their skills to discipline-based learning and to their lives. And through all of this work, their writing skills continue to develop. When I work with teachers, I often say to them, "If your students' writing skills are not visibly, dramatically improving after a few weeks of instruction, you are doing something wrong." Over all these years, it has become crystal clear to us that when teaching writing, *good* teaching pays off. When you provide students with constant opportunities to write and when you actively and assertively teach into their best efforts, their development as writers will astonish you, their parents, the school administrators, and best of all, the youngsters themselves.

It is not only *children's* work that is transformed when teachers are supported in the teaching of writing; *teachers'* work is also transformed. One of the beautiful things about teaching writing is that no one needs to make a choice between responsive, developmentally appropriate teaching and results-oriented, data-based teaching. The good news is that when children write, their thinking, their progress, and their vulnerabilities will inevitably be right there before your eyes—and before their eyes, too. Whereas reading must be translated into something that is no longer reading for it to be on the page, in black and white, growth in writing is always concrete, demonstrable, and evidenced-based.

Then, too, when a community of teachers embraces reform in the teaching of writing, teachers often become reinvigorated and renewed in the process. And individual teachers find that teaching writing taps new sources of energy within themselves. Over the years, teachers have continually told me that the teaching of writing has given them new energy, clarity, and compassion, reminding them why they went into teaching in the first place. I understand what these teachers mean, for writing has done all this—and more—for me.

All of this creates an escalating demand for professional development in writing.

THE SERIES: BOTH CURRICULUM *AND* PROFESSIONAL DEVELOPMENT

The Units of Study series has been written in ways that double as both curricular support and professional development. Each day's instruction is designed according to research-based principles. For example, you will see that one day after another, all of the teaching follows the "gradual release of responsibility" model of teaching. Students can first learn from a demonstration (accompanied by an explicit explanation), then from guided practice in which the amount of scaffolding they receive is lessened over time, and then from independent work, for which they receive feedback. Then, too, you'll see that when we first use a new method, it is a simplified and streamlined method. We take the time to coach students so they understand their role in that method. Over time, the method then becomes more layered and complex, fluid and implicit.

The progressions that you will see in our teaching are always carefully chosen and explicitly explained. Our goal is to highlight the replicable teaching moves in ways that allow you to transfer those same moves to curriculum that you invent. I know from helping thousands of teachers learn to teach writing that these units will scaffold and inform your own teaching, and you will develop finesse and flexibility with the methods and information conveyed in these books.

The wonderful thing about learning to teach writing well is that there are just a few teaching methods that one needs to know and be able to use. In this series, I provide crystal clear advice on how to lead efficient and effective minilessons, conferences, and small-group strategy sessions. I do so knowing that as you travel through the series, encountering scores of transcripts of minilessons, conferences, small-group sessions, and shares, you will learn not only from explicit instruction but also from immersion. This—the first book of the series—explicitly describes the architecture of all our minilessons, conferences, and small-group strategy sessions and details the management techniques that make writing workshops possible. *Writing Pathways: Performance Assessments and Learning Progressions, K–5* provides you with an assessment system that can make teaching and learning robust, goal-directed, data-based, and responsive. The subsequent books show these methods and principles affecting real-life classrooms.

Ideally, you and every other teacher in the world should be able not only to observe exemplary teachers but also to do so with a coach nearby, highlighting the way the teaching illustrates a collection of guiding principles. Therefore, as you witness my teaching and that of my colleagues, I will also be an ever-present coach, underscoring aspects of the teaching that seem especially essential. My goal is to help you watch this teaching in ways that enable you to extrapolate guidelines and methods, so that on another day you'll invent your own teaching. After all, these books provide a detailed model; they are not meant as a script. The end goal is not the teaching that we've described here but the teaching that you, your colleagues, and your children invent together.

AN OVERVIEW OF THE SERIES

This book—*A Guide to the Common Core Writing Workshop*—accompanies the series of books written for kindergarten teachers, for first-grade teachers, and also for second-grade teachers. (I've also written a similar guide for third-, fourth-, and fifth-grade teachers.) Each grade's series contains:

- The *Guide to the Common Core Writing Workshop*
- Four Common Core–aligned units of study, including one unit each in opinion, information, and narrative writing
- A book of alternate and additional units, the *If . . . Then . . . Curriculum: Assessment-Based Instruction*, written to help you differentiate curriculum
- A book that puts a system for assessing writing into your hands and into the hands of your students, *Writing Pathways: Performance Assessments and Learning Progressions, K–5*
- A CD-ROM, *Resources for Teaching Writing*, of additional resources, including paper choices, sample student writing, and reproducible checklists

The intent of this series is to support students' abilities to be strategic, metacognitive writers who use particular processes to achieve particular purposes as writers. Within a grade and across grades, the books fit tongue and groove alongside each other. Together, they help students consolidate and use what they have learned to do so that they meet and exceed the Common Core State Standards for each grade. More importantly, the books help students learn to use writing as a tool for learning across the day and throughout their richly literate lives.

Four Common Core–Aligned Unit of Study Books

Each unit of study book represents about six weeks of teaching, and within those six weeks, the unit supports a great many cycles of drafting and revision, as well as several publications. The units align with the types of writing that are predominant in the Common Core State Standards. For example, at each grade level, one or two of the unit of study books fall under the umbrella of opinion writing. In the kindergarten unit, *Persuasive Writing of All Kinds*, children write persuasive signs, letters, songs, and speeches. In first grade, they write persuasive reviews—including book reviews. And in second grade, students develop, support, and share their opinions as they write a variety of texts about their reading. In the same way, there are units at each grade level that support students' development in narrative. For example, in kindergarten, children write true stories, working to make sure those stories are in fact stories, and that they are readable by readers. In first grade, youngsters write Small Moment stories, working to make their characters come to life. In second grade, youngsters study the craft of narrative writing, writing under the tutelage of Jane Yolen and Angela Johnson. There are, in the same way, a series of grade-specific units supporting information writing.

Then, at every grade, there is a fourth book in addition to a book that supports each of the three types of writing that are highlighted in the CCSS. In kindergarten, the extra book is actually the launch—a book that teaches children how to participate in a writing workshop and how to write and that supports both information and story writing. In first grade, the extra book is a second narrative unit, this time teaching writers to write series fiction books; in second grade, this is a book on poetry and on reading-writing connections.

The books are written in a way that gives you the chance to listen in on and observe the unit being taught with students just the age of your students. It will be almost as if you were invited into a classroom to watch and listen as my coauthors and I work with kindergartners, first-graders, or second-graders. You will listen as we convene the class of children into the meeting area for a ten-minute minilesson, channeling them to sit beside partners and calling for their attention, and you'll hear how we talk about and demonstrate the strategies and skills of effective writing. Of course, you'll also overhear the jokes and stories we use to draw them in and the directions we give to send them off to their work time. Then, too, you'll hear the ways we confer and lead small groups to support the work they do during that day's workshop. You'll watch us teach writers to self-assess their writing early in a unit of study, becoming familiar with goals for that unit, and you'll see the way that learning progressions and data weave through every unit of study. You'll see pre- and postassessments bookend each unit of study.

That is, each of the four Unit of Study books contains the words of our teaching (and students' responses to it) for that entire six-week-long unit of study. We also provide representative examples of the writing youngsters did in each unit of study.

Each Day in a Unit of Study Book

Once you are teaching a unit, you will find that in each day's teaching, each *session* within that unit is introduced with a prelude that helps you to understand why, out of all that could possibly be taught at that juncture, we decided on that particular minilesson. The art of teaching comes from choice. The prelude, then, brings you in on the rationale behind the choices that inform the upcoming session. Why this minilesson? How will it fit with earlier and with later instruction? What are the real goals? The prelude highlights what matters most in the session, and hopefully it functions as a bit of a keynote speech, revving you up for the teaching that follows.

Then, you can listen in to state-of-the-art *minilessons*, taught to children who are just the age of your class. Hear the language that I (and coauthors) use, and hear some of the ways children respond. Each minilesson follows the same architecture, which is described in more detail in Chapter 7.

After we send students off to their work spots, my colleagues and I fill you in on the *conferring and small-group work* we are apt to do during the upcoming work time. More often than not, this section will be like a miniature workshop, teaching you ways to teach responsively. That teaching will be punctuated with *mid-workshop teaching* that we give to the whole class, partway through writing time. Often, this teaching builds upon the minilesson, extending it by providing a next step or a follow-up point. Sometimes the mid-workshop teaching counterbalances the minilesson or broadcasts lessons that are being taught in conferences or small groups. Either way, most mid-workshop teachings are actually mini-minilessons! We also describe the whole-class *share* session that culminates the workshop.

A Book of Alternate and Additional Units

For each grade level, in addition to the four units of study, we have written a grade-specific book titled *If . . . Then . . . Curriculum: Assessment-Based Instruction.*

Each of these books offers shortened versions of five to six grade-specific units of study that you might decide to teach before, after, or in between the core curriculum. For example, if you worry that your second-graders didn't participate in the first-grade unit on information writing—one that introduces nonfiction chapter books and teaching texts—you might conclude that they don't have the background they need to take the unit *Lab Reports and Science Books* by storm. In *If . . . Then . . . Curriculum: Assessment-Based Instruction*, you will receive practical help teaching a simple information unit that provides the most essential content from those units that your children missed. Similar help is given to support children who may not be ready for a mentor author study because they don't have prior experience in Common Core–aligned narrative writing. Then again, your second-graders may instead be chomping at the bit for additional challenges, and the *If . . . Then . . .* book provides you with detailed help teaching units in writing gripping stories and persuasive reviews, for example. In the same fashion, I've anticipated the challenges kindergarten and first-grade teachers face, suggesting, "If your data look like this . . . here's what I suggest. . . ."

The curriculum we've described in enormous detail only supports half or two thirds of your school year so you will want to teach these additional units of study.

A Book of Assessment Tools

The curriculum set out in these units is integrated into an assessment system that includes three learning progressions, one in each type of writing, as well as grade-by-grade checklists, grade-specific rubrics, and three benchmark texts illustrating at-standards-level, on-demand opinion, information, and narrative writing. An early version of this assessment system has been piloted in thousands of classrooms, and the entire system has been revised based on feedback.

Essentially, in this system, K–8 teachers begin the school year by asking students to spend forty-five minutes writing an on-demand narrative, and on other days, to spend similar time writing an on-demand information text and opinion text. In most schools, teachers decide that in each instance, students will merely be told to do their best writing. A teacher might say to her students, for example, "You have forty-five minutes to write your best personal narrative, Small Moment story, true story, or piece of short fiction—your best narrative. Write in a way that shows me all you know about narrative writing." Some schools prefer the prompt to be much more clearly delineated, with all the expectations spelled out, and we provide schools with both ways to word the tasks so you may choose the method you prefer.

Each student's work is then scored against a learning progression and an accompanying set of sample student texts in each genre that have been benchmarked to represent each level of the learning progression. For example, a reader can read the introduction in one child's information text, asking, "Does this match expectations for a first-grade introduction? A second-grade introduction? A third-grade one?" (There is also a way for teachers to characterize the piece as 2.5 or 3.5.) Then, teachers teach the class of students a unit on information writing, giving students ample opportunities to assess themselves at the beginning, middle, and end of the unit against crystal clear checklists that spell out the goals they should be working toward. After the unit is completed, the on-demand assessment is repeated, and students' work is again scored. Presumably, teachers will teach more than one unit in each of the three major kinds of writing, and the on-demands can be given periodically again later in the year to continue to track students' progress.

The most important thing about the learning progressions and performance assessments is that they enable teachers and students to grasp where students are in their writing development so that teachers can figure out ways to give children the help they need to move toward next steps. The assessment system that undergirds this curriculum is meant as an instructional tool. It makes progress in writing as transparent, concrete, and obtainable as possible and puts ownership for this progress into the hands of learners. As part of this, this system of assessment demystifies the Common Core State Standards, allowing students and teachers to work toward a very clear image of what good writing entails.

A CD-ROM of Additional Resources

The accompanying CD-ROM offers print resources as well as student samples. On the CD-ROM, you'll find paper choices, reproducible checklists and rubrics, editing checklists, and conferring scenarios (from the *If . . .*

Then . . . book) that can be printed on label paper so you can leave your students with an artifact of your teaching. These resources will support your teaching throughout the year.

The Series Components All Together: A PreK–6 Learning Progression

If you are truly going to bring all of your students to the ambitious standards of the CCSS, there needs to be vertical alignment in the curriculum so that people who teach at any grade level can count on students entering their classrooms with some foundational skills that can then be built upon. The days of each teacher functioning as a Lone Ranger in the teaching of writing are at an end. Imagine how impractical it would be if each first-grade teacher decided whether to teach addition; second-grade teachers who received students from several different first grades would find that half the class had never learned anything about addition, and the other half was chomping at the bit to study multidigit addition and subtraction! Of course, almost every school *does* have a math curriculum that supports vertical alignment. Granted, even in a school where students are all taught properties of addition and subtraction in first grade, some students won't master those skills; still, there is agreement that a shared math curriculum means that teachers can extend and build upon previous instruction. Until the release of the Common Core State Standards, many educators didn't realize that writing skills, too, need to develop incrementally, with the work that students do at one grade level standing on the shoulders of prior learning.

In this series, instruction builds on itself. Often that instruction may have occurred in a different genre, within that same school year. For example, a teacher might say, "In your earlier unit of study in narrative writing, you learned that writers include the specific words that characters say. Today I want to teach you that including the exact words that people say is also important when writing a speech." In this way, you bring students to higher levels of achievement by making sure that your teaching stands on the shoulders of prior instruction.

Sometimes the prior instruction that undergirds a minilesson will have occurred during the previous year. "I know that last year you learned that when writing about information, it helps to group your writing into sections. Last year, most of you grouped your writing into chapters, each addressing a different subtopic. This year, I want to tell you it is important to include a few sentences within your introductory paragraph that let readers know the plan for how you will group the information, for how those subsections will go."

Of course, teaching involves not only a well-planned curriculum, but also deep assessment and responsive instruction. Students will be able to proceed up the vertical alignment in the series only if teachers use, and make teaching decisions based on, the assessments in this series. These assessments scaffold the curriculum and are also aligned both with the Common Core State Standards and with preceding grade levels' work. For example, the CCSS state that in second grade, writers must be able to introduce their topic and provide a concluding statement or section for their informational writing (W.2.3). In the Unit of Study learning progressions, teachers can see ways to teach students to do this, and they can see how those techniques relate to what was taught in the preceding years. Using a rubric based on the learning progression for narrative writing, teachers can collect data that reveal which students still need help with that foundational skill, and they can alter their teaching accordingly.

WHAT'S CHANGED IN THIS NEW SERIES?

This series is not a second edition of the original Units of Study for Primary Writing. It is a set of mostly (and sometimes entirely) new books.

The New Series Is Grade Specific

The biggest difference between this series and the former series is that the units of study are now grade specific. This means, for example, that the kindergarten series tells about teaching in kindergarten classrooms. The first kindergarten unit acknowledges that most children will be labeling their drawings—and the letters in those labels will include squiggles and diamonds. The second unit helps children write true stories—but does so with full awareness that the hard part will be writing readable words. Growth in kindergarten is spectacular, and by the later kindergarten units, children are invited to use their newfound powers to live writerly lives, writing how-to

"This assessment system makes progress transparent, concrete, and obtainable; puts ownership for progress into the hands of learners; and demystifies the Common Core State Standards."

texts and writing petitions, persuasive letters, and signs that rally people to address problems in the classroom, the school, and the world. We emphasize the writerly life in kindergarten because we want youngsters to learn not only how to write, but why one writes.

The first-grade series is written for children who are just tapping into their burgeoning powers as readers, as well as writers, and (with your help) come to believe they can do anything. They'll write Small Moment stories, of course, since no unit has captured the imagination of teachers and of children more than this one. They'll also write nonfiction chapter books, persuasive reviews, and a whole series of fiction books, modeled after Henry and Mudge.

The second-grade series is written with seven-year-olds in mind. These youngsters are chomping at the bit for something new. They feel very big now and want work that feels big and important. That's what they'll get; the series invites second-graders into author studies that help them to craft powerful true stories; science investigations and lab reports; poetry that requires CCSS reading as well as writing work; nominations for the best book, the most powerful character, the worst bad guy, the best descriptive writing, and countless other awards; and, as part of that, into some very grown-up writing-about-reading work.

Throughout the units, we've written not only with a specific grade level in mind, but also with a specific time of year in mind. After all, the difference between the beginning and end of kindergarten can be just about as big as the difference between third grade and high school. And second-graders come into the year writing a few sentences per page in their illustrated booklets, and they leave able to write page-long drafts in a single sitting! The primary units of study, then, are very different depending on if they are written for fall or for spring.

Because these units are written for specific grade levels, one unit is able to stand on the shoulders of the preceding unit. That is, the first-grade unit on writing fiction helps youngsters to recall and apply the knowledge they learned in a *Small Moments* unit at the start of that year. There are references to prior years' instruction, too, and we hope and expect that usually, these units will be taught as part of a coherent program of study. The *If . . . Then . . . Curriculum: Assessment-Based Instruction* book will help those of you whose children have not had prior instruction know how to alter your teaching accordingly.

The New Series Takes Up the Challenges of the CCSS for Writing and Exceeds Them

Of course, much of the impetus for this new series was the nation's widespread adoption of the Common Core State Standards. For those of us who know and love the writing workshop, it seems as if many aspects of the writing standards have been written with a writing workshop precisely in mind. The grade-by-grade standards fit our understanding of how young people develop within a writing workshop. To those of us who know the fingerprints of writing workshop instruction, it is clear that many of the exemplar texts in the appendix emerged from workshops.

However, the arrival of the CCSS has challenged even writing workshop advocates to develop more sequential, ambitious work in opinion/argument writing and in writing across the curriculum. We've responded to this wise challenge by developing a sequential, K–5 curriculum in opinion/argument and information writing and by giving renewed attention to particular kinds of writing about reading and writing across the curriculum. (Mary Ehrenworth, Chris Lehman, and I have written a book detailing our thinking about the CCSS and the implications for teachers and for curriculum, *Pathways to the Common Core* [2012], which I invite you to read for a more detailed discussion of this topic.) We've also taken priorities of the Common Core Standards and imbued them into all our work, including an emphasis on close reading, text-based questioning, data-based instruction, reading like a writer, writing about texts, quick writes, and transference.

The Teachers College Reading and Writing Project is especially embedded in schools within New York State, which means that frameworks New York State has adopted for accelerating achievement toward CCSS levels are part and parcel of these units. This includes:

- Attention to the level of cognitive challenge we provide students using Webb's depth of knowledge as a guide

- Reliance on curricular mapping design strategies
- Attention to Charlotte Danielson's teacher-effectiveness framework
- A focus on formative and summative assessments and data-based instruction

The work your students will do as you teach the units of study in this series and as you track and support their progress on the learning progressions that undergird this curriculum will provide them with the instruction, opportunities for practice, and goals they need to meet the CCSS for writing at their grade level. In fact, since we believe it is so important for every child to be able to meet those standards, we have made sure that every yearlong curriculum teaches students in ways that support standards-level work at the level *above* their grade level. This allows for accelerated progress for students who can make that progress and for extra time and scaffolding for those who need this to become proficient at the grade-level standard.

Because the units of study at each grade level support students to work within the standards of the upcoming grade, these units of study support children becoming highly proficient while also allowing youngsters who need more teaching and more practice to receive those extended opportunities to learn while still achieving proficiency. The units, then, help teachers and students to aim not only for grade-level standards but also beyond them. Runners don't aim to stop at the finish line; they aim to run right through it, keeping up the pace until the finish line is well behind them. We too want to aim beyond the finish line, bringing every child with us as we do so.

Although this series does not take on the entire job of helping students meet the Common Core Reading, Speaking and Listening, and Language Standards, good writing instruction requires meeting many of these standards all the same, and you'll find the units help you do this. You'll see CCSS correlation charts aligned to each unit that will help you understand which of these other sets of standards these units help you meet and which will especially need attention in other times of day—in social studies or science, reading, and language/word study. The good news is that the work students do across the entire curriculum will be given a lift by the skills they develop within the writing workshop.

I discuss the CCSS in more depth in the next chapter.

This New Series Reflects Current Research and Knowledge

Since we published the first Units of Study series, knowledge of education has changed. The work of Danielson, Marzano, Webb, Wiggins, Hattie, and others has coalesced into new images and understandings of effective practice. Teachers are being assessed with new lenses in mind. Students' progress is now tracked with preassessments, formative assessments, and summative assessments. Somehow, all of that assessing must be synthesized into instruction that is more rigorous and more powerful than ever—and that means the instruction needs to be more assessment-based and data driven as well as more cognitively demanding than ever.

Over the past few years, the Teachers College Reading and Writing Project has been the primary vehicle for professional development in more than a thousand schools, including both high-need schools and high-performing private, charter, and public schools. These partnership mean that we regularly help schools undergo quality review, develop and adopt CCSS–aligned performance assessments, use software systems to track student progress, and demonstrate to evaluators that instruction is data-based and differentiated. Our deep involvement with all of this work has helped our own ideas evolve. The fruits of that labor are infused into these units of study.

THE AUTHORSHIP OF THIS SERIES

Although the text reads as if one teacher created and taught the minilessons, mid-workshops, small groups, and shares, the creation and teaching was actually much more collaborative. Usually, before embarking on a project, the coauthors and I will have designed and taught scores, even hundreds, of units of study related to the topic of the unit book. Usually the work began with the coauthor and me working hard to develop a tentative plan for the entire unit. Implicit in such a document are literally hundreds of decisions, and our initial plans were always revised endlessly before becoming the backbone of the unit. During the early planning portion of the process, we'd decide on mentor texts and the like. Then, I'd usually draft the first few minilessons, and the coauthor would pilot those minilessons in a few classrooms, and we'd work together to revise them. Then one of us would draft the bare bones of the next sessions, and again, others would chip in. The initial draft of the first bend usually went through four or five wholesale revisions, was taught several times, and was passed among a number of hands before it was close to being finished. Once the first bend had been written and taught, plans for the upcoming bend would be revised based on all that we'd learned, and then the process continued. I ended up revising at least half the books from head to toe again, later in the process.

In the same way, although the books read as if they draw on one classroom, depicting the true story of how that unit of study unfolded in that one classroom, in truth, the classroom that is depicted in these books is usually a composite classroom, and the kids' voices are captured or created from all the kids we've taught.

The series, then, stands on the shoulders of the Teachers College Reading and Writing Project community. The books have, in a sense, been coauthored by the entire staff of this professional development organization and by the children, teachers, principals, and superintendents who have become part of the community of practice, helping develop, pilot, and revise the ideas that fill the pages of these books.

Chapter 2

What Do the CCSS Say about Writing, and What Does This Mean for Us?

THIS SERIES is being published just as the United States sets out to lift the level of literacy instruction across all our schools, making sure that students enter college and twenty-first-century careers ready to flourish. As I've written about in our recent professional book *Pathways to the Common Core*, the Common Core State Standards are a big deal. Adopted by forty-five states and the District of Columbia so far, the standards represent the most sweeping reform of the K–12 curriculum that has ever occurred in this country. It is safe to say that across the entire history of American education, no single document has played a more influential role over what is taught in our schools. The standards are already shaping what is published, mandated, and tested in schools—and also what is marginalized and neglected. Any educator who wants to play a role in shaping what happens in schools, therefore, needs a deep understanding of these standards.

If I were asked to describe the two or three most striking features of the Common Core State Standards, one of the things I'd say straight away is that the standards place a tremendous emphasis on writing. In effect, the standards refocus the nation on students' proficiency as writers. NCLB, the last large-scale reform movement in literacy, called for an emphasis on phonemic awareness, phonics, vocabulary, fluency, and comprehension. Writing was nowhere in the picture. In the Common Core State Standards, in contrast, writing is treated as an equal partner to reading, and more than this, writing is assumed to be the vehicle through which a great deal of the critical thinking, reading work, and reading assessment will occur. The CCSS, then, return writing to its place as one of the essentials of education.

In this chapter, I help you grasp the Common Core's rallying cry around writing and help you understand how these units of study help you meet (and even, at times, exceed) these demands. This chapter looks specifically at:

- The standards' emphasis on three types of writing
- The relationship between the CCSS for writing and the Units of Study series

- The writing process described in the standards and taught in these units of study
- The standards' call for new levels of proficiency

In subsequent chapters in this guide, you'll see how the structure, focus, and content of the units align to—and are influenced by—the Common Core State Standards. You'll see the influence of the Common Core also as you read the individual lessons that lead students toward and beyond CCSS benchmarks.

THE STANDARDS' EMPHASIS ON THREE TYPES OF WRITING

In the prelude to the Common Core Standards, there is a section entitled "Key Features of the Standards" (8). This synopsis emphasizes that although the writing process applies to all kinds of writing, different types of writing place different demands on students.

The standards are organized in a way that highlights grade-specific expectations for three broad types of writing. The first standard delineates expectations for opinion and argument writing; the second, for information writing; the third, for narrative writing. Although these three standards represent just under a third of the ten standards, if one were to count the pages devoted to the writing standards and count the pages devoted to explicating the three types of writing, one would find that these first three standards occupy fully half of the CCSS for writing. (The later standards illuminate how students should do the work of the first three standards. For example, students presumably will use the writing process detailed in standard 5, the writing process standard, as they write the argument, information, and narrative texts described in standards 1–3.)

It is interesting to note that the standards refer to these as *types* of writing, not as *genres*. This makes sense because within any one type of writing, one can lodge many different genres of writing. In the New Standards Project, an earlier effort to create nationwide standards, the committee of twenty (including me) who wrote those standards wrestled with the issue of *kinds* versus *structures* versus *types* versus *genres* of writing and came to the decision that the whole world of writing could be divided into five (not three) *kinds*

of writing: narrative, information, functional and procedural, persuasion and argument, and poetry. The Common Core Standards' divisions are roughly in line with those earlier ones, although functional and procedural writing are now combined with information writing, and poetry is excluded.

You might, with colleagues, try jotting down the genres you would put under these major categories and then consider how often your students have opportunities to engage in each of the three main types of writing. You will probably come up with lists like these.

- **Narrative writing:** personal narrative, fiction, historical fiction, fantasy, narrative memoir, biography, narrative nonfiction
- **Persuasive/opinion/argument writing:** persuasive letter, petition, persuasive speech, review, personal essay, persuasive essay, literary essay, historical essay, editorial, op-ed column, research-based argument essay
- **Informational and functional/procedural writing:** how-to book, directions, recipe, lab report, fact sheet, news article, feature article, blog, website, report, analytic memo, research report, nonfiction book

The CCSS and Narrative Texts

Although the sequence of the first three anchor standards for writing starts with argument writing and ends with narrative writing, learners grow into these genres in just the opposite direction. Human beings grow up on narratives, on stories. We come to know our own parents by hearing their stories of growing up. We make friendships by sharing the stories of our lives. We get jobs and scholarships by telling the stories of our studies and careers. We stay in touch by regaling each other with the news of our comings and goings. We plan and daydream and work and worry in narrative; we recall and remember in narrative. We comprehend fiction and biography and narrative nonfiction by synthesizing what we read on one page, another, and another into narratives that we hope are coherent and satisfying.

Narratives are important not only because they are, as researcher Barbara Hardy says, the primary mode of knowing ("Narrative as a Primary Act of Mind" in *The Cool Web: The Patterns of Children's Reading*, 1977), but also because they are an essential component in almost every other kind of writing.

Listen to TED talks—models of persuasive and informative speaking—and you will find that mostly, those speeches are mosaics of stories. Read a terrific informational text, and you'll find that you are reading stories.

If you try to understand the narrative writing standards by turning immediately to the grade you teach and reading the descriptors for that grade, you'll probably find the expectations to be overwhelming. Before you dismiss the standards as unrealistically high, you need to read them in an entirely different fashion. Start with kindergarten, and read those grade-level skills for narrative. Imagine a very simple story that meets those descriptors. Then reread just the first subitem in the kindergarten narrative standard before looking to the right to note what added work first-graders are expected to do in narrative writing. The added work won't be much—and that will prove true as you progress step by step through narrative expectations. By proceeding in this way, reading in a horizontal fashion, setting the descriptors for each skill from one grade alongside those for the next grade and noting the new work that is added at each subsequent grade, you'll come to understand the trajectory along which writers can travel. It is this trajectory that we used when designing the narrative units found in this series (and it is the information and opinion trajectories that we used for the information and opinion units). Using these incremental steps, this trajectory will, in fact, make the writing standards something that students will be able to achieve, especially if they have the opportunity to grow up within a strong writing curriculum.

The CCSS and Opinion/Argument Texts

Argument writing is a *big deal* in the Common Core State Standards. In fact, the writers include an entire section in Appendix A titled "The Special Place of Argument in the Standards" (24) to emphasize their strong belief in argumentation. The section begins, "While all three text types are important,

"You might want to consider how often your students have opportunities to engage in each of the three main types of writing: narrative, persuasive/opinion/ argument and informational/ functional/procedural."

the Standards put particular emphasis on students' ability to write sound arguments on substantive topics and issues, as this ability is critical to college and career readiness." To support their argument, the authors refer to statements by college professors who each make additional claims for the centrality of argument in universities. Gerald Graff, for example, claims that the university is largely "an argument culture" (*Clueless in Academe*, 2003, 24). It is with this particular vision of university life that the standards writers mapped their expectations for argument writing from high school graduation backward.

It seems important to note that this belief in the essential nature of argumentation, at least on the part of the writers of the standards, colors many areas of the CCSS document. There is a push for logical reasoning, analysis of claims, and reliance on clear evidence and evaluation of sources throughout the document.

The pace at which the opinion and argument standards develop is brisk when you study them longitudinally. Kindergarten and first grade begin simply enough, expecting a student to introduce a topic and supply some opinion for it, perhaps with a reason. But then in second grade, the student is already expected to structure his or her writing in support of his or her claim. In fact, in some respects, the expectations for second-grade argument writing, at least in terms of the text of the standards, seems to outpace that of the other two writing types. In second-grade information writing, the main emphasis seems to be only that the text includes a variety of details, whereas the expectations for argument writing are more extensive.

There are three important ideas that will help you study the Common Core standards for argument writing: the continuum of expectations for opinion and argument writing is steep; the K–5 emphasis on opinion writing gives way to a 6–12 emphasis on argument writing (which includes counterargument and more critical weighing of sources, evidence, and logic); and writing arguments eventually includes using and evaluating sources, and using this analysis to power convincing arguments. The opinion and argument units in this series support this full progression of skills so that students develop research-based argument writing skills in fifth grade.

The CCSS and Information Texts

To understand the Common Core State Standards for information writing, it is helpful to pause for a moment and think of all the information writing that students do in school. Although research reports and nonfiction books spring to mind right away, this category of writing is far broader than that. Information writing includes entries, Post-it® notes, summaries written in response to reading, lab reports, math records, and descriptions of and reflections on movies, field trips, and books. Under the umbrella of the broad category one also finds the answers students write in response to questions at the end of textbook chapters, or questions discussed in class. The CCSS authors highlight the breadth of this type of writing in Appendix A.

> Informational/explanatory writing includes a wide array of genres, including academic genres such as literary analyses, scientific and historical reports, summaries, and précis writing as well as forms of workplace and functional writing such as instructions, manuals, memos, reports, applications, and résumés. (23)

In essence, the skills required to write information texts are not just writing skills, they are learning skills.

Let's clarify something before diving much further into this topic: although the rhetoric around the Common Core suggests that the standards call for exponentially increasing the amount of information writing done in a school, this depends on the amount of writing teachers have done all along. The truth is that for teachers in grades K–5, the Common Core Standards ask only that one third of all the writing that students do across the entire day be information writing. That is, most of the writing in science, social studies, art, and computers all qualifies as information writing.

We think it's important to note that for many schools, the challenge is not the expectation that students devote a greater percentage of their writing to texts that fall under the broad umbrella of information writing (it is already commonplace for one third of the writing that students do to be information writing). Rather, the challenge is that the Common Core expects students to apply the same standard of craftsmanship to information writing as they do to short stories, memoirs, and essays. That is, traditionally, when students write about reading (whether literature or history or science), the goal has been for them to show that they have done the reading, gleaned the necessary knowledge, and developed some thoughts. Prior to the arrival of the CCSS, it wasn't usual for their information writing to be held up to the same standards as essays and short stories. Now, a reader of the CCSS can quickly see that across all three kinds of writing, there is a parallel emphasis on writing in clear structures, on elaborating with specific information, on writing with details and examples, and on synthesizing the text so that the entire text advances key ideas or themes.

THE RELATIONSHIP BETWEEN THE CCSS FOR WRITING AND THE UNITS OF STUDY SERIES

The standards, you'll recall, focus on expectations and not methods. They detail what students should know and be able to do; they do not specify practices that teachers should use to teach students the skills they need to meet those expectations. School districts and teachers are left to decide on an instructional program that will elevate the level of student writing so that all (or most) students reach these ambitious expectations. One can't help but think that an effort to meet the standards will require a planned, sequential, explicit writing program, with instruction that gives students repeated opportunities to practice each kind of writing and to receive explicit feedback at frequent intervals.

This new series offers one such program. The units of study in this series offer at least one highly developed unit devoted to each type of writing for each grade level. Within each unit of study, students are expected to write more than one piece (and sometimes a score of pieces). The fact that students are given repeated opportunities to produce a particular kind of writing is important if we are going to hold students accountable to meeting CCSS expectations. For anyone to become highly skilled at a type of writing, that person needs opportunities for repeated practice. In this series, these opportunities are given not only within a unit of study but also across units of study and grades.

Progression and Transference across Units and Grades

Across all of the units, there is a continual emphasis on transference. For example, after students write persuasive speeches, they study another kind of persuasive writing—petitions—and ask, "How many of the strategies that we learned when writing persuasive speeches are also applicable when writing petitions?" This inquiry leads students to plunge right into the work of writing petitions without needing an elaborate introduction. The very design of the Common Core emphasizes the fact that students will be able to reach high-level expectations when skills are built upon as students proceed up the grades. In this series, the cohesion across units means that skills that are introduced in one grade level are then recalled, and developed in, later units of study.

This development occurs within a type of writing and also across the full gamut of kinds of writing. That is, the standards' expectations for one type of writing, at a grade level, are echoed in other types of writing. If students are expected to end their essays by referring back not only to the last paragraph but to their entire essay, they'll encounter parallel expectations for their endings when writing narratives and information texts. It is helpful for students if teachers say, "You know the work you have been doing to make sure that the ending of your essay relates to the whole text, not just to the last bit of it? Well, when you write fiction, there are similar expectations for your endings. Let me explain and show you what I mean."

You will want to study the standards so that you understand the way that expectations grow each year, with students being expected, each year, to produce work that stands on the shoulders of the preceding year. For example, first-graders are expected to write opinion pieces in which they introduce the topic of the book they are writing about, state an opinion, supply a reason to support that opinion, and provide some sense of closure. By sixth grade, students are expected to write arguments (not opinions) to support claims with clear reasons and relevant evidence. In these arguments, students are expected to introduce the claim(s) and organize the reasons and evidence clearly; support claim(s) with clear reasons and relevant evidence, using credible sources in a way that demonstrates an understanding of the topic or text; use words, phrases, and clauses to clarify the relationships among claims and reasons; establish a formal style; and provide a concluding statement or section that follows from the argument presented.

> "The CCSS emphasize that writing needs to occur in disciplines and be supported by all teachers."

The standards not only describe the progression of skill development that is expected to occur across grades in a curriculum in which one grade builds upon the next, they also provide annotated exemplar texts to illustrate what these pieces of writing might look like and to answer the question, "How good is good enough?" When looking at the pieces that are provided as illustrations of one type of writing or another, it is important to note that even the pieces selected as exemplars do not adhere to all of the defining characteristics of a genre. For readers who are accustomed to teaching in writing workshops, it will be clear to you, after just a glance, that most of the exemplar pieces in Appendix B emerged out of writing workshop classrooms.

Exemplar pieces are important, and although the standards include a random sampling of some exemplars, they don't show information, opinion, and narrative pieces that illustrate each of the standards they detail. This series does provide those benchmark texts in *Writing Pathways: Performance Assessments and Learning Progressions, K–5*. Of course, once you teach these units, you will have files of student work from previous years that you can draw upon, and you will want to do so.

If you are by any chance operating in isolation, a sort of lone champion of writing in your school, I encourage you to reach out in every possible way to your colleagues. Your influence on one class of writers will be multiplied tenfold if students receive instruction each year that builds on prior years, makes sense to them, and holds them accountable to transferring and applying their skills. To reach the Common Core Standards, children will benefit from writing becoming a schoolwide vision.

Writing across the Curriculum

Although the expectations for writing that are embedded in the CCSS mostly align to the research and teaching that the Teachers College Reading and Writing Project has been engaged with for the past thirty years, there have been important new challenges as well. First and foremost, the CCSS emphasize that writing needs to occur in disciplines and be supported by all teachers. Writing cannot be the province only of the language arts classroom. As part of this, the CCSS spotlight the importance of high standards for the writing that is done within the content areas. Children need to be able to structure their research reports, to synthesize information, to explore the ramifications of evidence. This means that young people need explicit instruction and lots of opportunities to write within social studies and science, and to develop as writers of information and opinion texts. This series contains research-based units that are embedded in the content areas as well as in the writing workshop.

A word about balance. The standards not only define and describe the three kinds of writing and show how students' work with each of those kinds of writing should progress across the years, but they also call for a distribution of writing experiences that gives students roughly equal amounts of time and instruction in argument, informational, and narrative writing.

In the Common Core, the discussion of the distribution of writing between these types of texts is situated under the subheading of "Shared Responsibility" (4) as part of an emphasis on writing instruction belonging in the hands of all disciplines and every teacher. That is, if fifth-grade students are expected to write narratives 35% of the time, information texts 35% of the time, and opinions/arguments 30% of the time, the balance between the three types of writing is expected to occur across math, social studies, science, gym, and music, as well as during writing workshop itself. Presumably, a good deal of the information writing will occur in science (lab reports), in math (math journals reflecting on the students' processes), in social studies (summaries of texts read, responses to questions asking students to synthesize information from several sources), and in reading (reading notebook entries, quick analytic jottings, preparations for partnership and book club conversations). This suggests that the CCSS recommend that a large portion of the writing done during the literacy or language arts block be narrative and opinion writing, although in this series, we support an equal distribution between the three types of writing.

The implications of the writing standards are clear. Writing must become part of the bill of rights for all students. Just as it would be unacceptable for a K–5 teacher to say, "Math's not really my thing," so too, in the world of the Common Core, it will be indefensible for a teacher, of any subject, to say, "Writing is not really my cup of tea."

Teaching to and above the Standards

Throughout the series, you will see that the teaching often reflects standards that are one grade level above. There are several reasons for this. First, teaching beyond the standards gives students the opportunity to reach toward the goal of working at highly proficient levels. Then too, as described previously, this means that students have additional time, when needed, to develop the skills they are expected to demonstrate. And finally, our research in thousands of writing classrooms has suggested to us that there are some places where the Common Core Standards underestimate what K–4 students can do. This is especially true in the primary grades, where the writing standards progress more slowly than in the upper grades. This means that there are instances in which expectations accelerate at a rate that we believe is unrealistically steep—most notably between sixth and seventh grade. Our suggestion, then, is for K–5 teachers to aim to send students to sixth grade already having met many of the sixth-grade standards. This positions students to leave eighth grade meeting or exceeding CCSS expectations.

THE WRITING PROCESS DESCRIBED IN THE STANDARDS AND TAUGHT IN THESE UNITS OF STUDY

While there is some dispute in this nation about methods for teaching *reading*, there is less dispute about methods for teaching *writing*. This is probably because while we don't have many public figures who are readers, there have been thousands of writers who have made their process public. There is near universal agreement that writers engage in a process of collecting, drafting, revising, and editing. You can see writers' drafts, with their many revisions, in library collections, online, and in books such as the Authors at Work series. From Mark Twain to Bob Woodward, from novelists to journalists, writers draft and revise—sometimes rapidly and on the run and sometimes over extended periods. It's no surprise, then, that the Standards embrace this widely accepted process.

Writing standard 5 describes the writing process, and standard 10 describes the need to write routinely as part of that process. Both standards will be an integral part of attaining all the other writing standards as well. The grade-level specifics of anchor standard 5 are almost the same across all the grades.

This standard says that students should be able to "develop and strengthen writing as needed by planning, revising, [and] editing" (18), with expectations for revision and independence increasing with age. Anchor standard 10 calls for students to "write routinely over extended time frames (time for research, reflection, and revision) and shorter time frames (a single sitting or a day or two)" (18). These are not low expectations! You'll find, as you dive deeper into these units, that tremendous attention is paid to on-demand writing at the start and end of each unit and on students producing a volume of writing. Writing with velocity matters, as does writing to deadline.

Efficiency and fluency also matter. These skills come with writing often, which the standards call for students to do. "Write routinely" means to make writing a habit. Even noted writers describe how they have to push themselves to ensure that they write every day. Novelist Margaret Atwood, who has published dozens of fiction and nonfiction books and has received almost every known award for her writing, claims, "The fact is the blank pages inspire me with terror. What will I put on them? Will it be good enough? Will I have to throw it out? The trick is to sit at the desk anyway, every day" (Donald Murray, *Shoptalk: Learning to Write with Writers*, 1990). It is not surprising that the standards emphasize writing often. Writing is just like any other practice—playing piano, running, knitting. The more opportunity you have for practice, the better you get. In these units, a day does not go by where your children are not writing. Across a week, they will write many pages. Inevitably, they will get better, faster, more fluent, more efficient, and more powerful.

A writing routine does not just come with sitting down to write, however. A writing routine involves understanding what it means to work at your writing. Writing anchor standard 5 states that writers will "develop and strengthen writing as needed by planning, revising, editing, rewriting, or trying a new approach" (18). The CCSS are closely aligned, then, with the practices researched by Pulitzer prize–winning journalist Don Murray, documented in *A Writer Teaches Writing* (2003). Murray described how journalists learn, even when writing to deadline, to revise on the run, to try out different leads and endings, and to consider and reconsider each word, comma, and sentence structure to convey precise meaning: they know that writing is a process.

Volume is also related to rate, and the standards are very specific about the expectations for production. Fourth-graders are expected to produce a minimum of one typed page in a sitting, and fifth-graders, a minimum of two typed pages in a sitting. We have seen students sit down to write an on-demand piece at the end of a unit of study and regularly produce that much writing. When they know a lot about what they are writing about, their pencils will fly. When they are used to writing often, their fingers and minds will be ready. That level of production requires practice.

This has led teachers to look closely at their schedules for writing, following a student across a week, seeing how much time is actually available for that student to write, and paying attention to how much writing that student actually produces during one sitting. In every school where kids become powerful writers, they have extended time to write, and they write daily. Don Graves, pioneer reformer in writing instruction for children, often said that if writers couldn't return to a piece of writing at least three times a week, it wasn't worth doing at all. The kids would just be too far away from their writing to remain committed to it (*Writing: Teachers and Children at Work*, 2003).

If you've ever practiced piano scales, you know that when you first sit down after a long stretch away from the piano, your fingers are slow. It's the same if you haven't exercised in a while or if you haven't picked up knitting needles in five years. You know the skills, but your legs or fingers don't respond with the speed you expected. On the other hand, as you begin to knit or run or play piano or write, you'll find that for every day you do it, the sheer discipline of moving your pen across the page, or your fingers across the keyboard, you will become faster and more fluent.

A note about typing versus handwriting: in most schools, students are writing on paper, not computers, because computers are expensive. You'll see that most of the K–5 student pieces that are in Appendix C of the standards are handwritten. That said, if your students have easy access to technology, it is important to help them develop those skills. It appears upcoming high-stake assessments will be conducted on the computer. You'll see, in the units of study, publishing options include podcasts, blogs, and other digital media, but ultimately, we've left the decision to highlight digital technology mostly in your hands.

THE STANDARDS' CALL FOR NEW LEVELS OF PROFICIENCY

The CCSS are notable in that they call for an equal division of time between three kinds of writing and for frequent opportunities to engage in the writing process. But the most remarkable thing about the CCSS is the call for high levels of proficiency. The expectations are not high for the younger grades, but they escalate between grades 5 and 8. In grade 5, the lead paragraph to a narrative story should "orient the reader by establishing a situation and introducing a narrator and/or characters; organize an event sequence that unfolds naturally" (20). So the writer is supposed to introduce the conflict and its context, introduce the narrator and the characters, and launch a sequence of events. And all of that just describes the opening few lines to a story! Many teachers no doubt think, "Could I write like that, with that much power and concision, let alone teach an eleven-year-old to write like that?" The expectations are especially high when one looks at the eighth-grade sample texts included in Appendix C.

Let's look at an example of a piece of writing from Appendix C that represents what kindergartners should be able to do as information writers:

To day befor We had riyda groos Mrs. John red us a strorry a baowt frogs. We had to riet a baowt frogs. We haf a tadpol in the sciens sentr. It has 2 bac ligs and wen it has 2 frunt ligs its tal disuprs and it can not yet wen its moot is chajn. Then the scknn gets to little and the frogs pol off thrr scknn an thaa eyt it. Saum of the frogs bloo baubools. Frogs lad eggs that look like jele and the fish yet some but some hach to tadpoos. It gros bigr and bigr and bigr.

The child has drawn on multiple sources of information, including observation and a text that was read aloud. The writer uses detail ("when it has 2 front legs its tail disappears") and precise and even domain-specific language (*tadpole, hatch*) to describe the life cycle of a frog. The writer makes comparisons ("eggs that look like jelly"), and uses repetition for dramatic effect ("bigger and bigger and bigger").

The pieces in the appendix are not all of even quality. Sometimes one type of writing at a grade level will represent what we might think are relatively low standards, while another piece, like this one, seems high. You'll need to look between the descriptors, the grade-level specifics in the standards—which tend to be rather low, especially in kindergarten and through fourth grade—and the pieces themselves, to try to build a coherent vision of proficiency levels if you're interested in doing this work. By the end of the year, you should be able to create your own Appendix C, with student exemplars from your community and curriculum.

The expectations for writing in the CCSS are also carried by anchor standard 4. At every grade level, starting in grade 3, standard 4 says that students are expected to "produce clear and coherent writing in which the development and organization are appropriate to task, purpose, and audience" (18). Note that a spotlight is placed on clarity and structure, as opposed to vividness or voice. This is interesting to us because we have often felt that one can look at various theories about writing instruction and ask, "Does this prioritize the sort of lush writing one finds in picture books, novels, and poems, or does it prioritize the lucid, clear writing that one finds in William Strunk and E. B. White's *Elements of Style*?" The CCSS lean toward the latter.

The Standards' Emphasis on the Importance of Writing for Very Young Students

Although this guide is for upper elementary grade teachers, the CCSS message to K–2 teachers matters to you. For you to do your job, it is important that writing instruction in your school starts in kindergarten. In thousands of schools across the nation, teachers start the kindergarten year by saying to children, "In this classroom, each one of you will be an author. Each one of you will write stories and letters and instructions and songs and all-about books." Although this teaching has spread like wildfire, it is still far from the norm. In the majority of classrooms, kindergarten is a time for socialization, for learning the alphabet, for perhaps copying the whole-class text, with an emphasis on penmanship. The Common Core State Standards convey a crystal clear message opposed to this practice. The message is this: kindergartners can write. They can not only invent their own spellings and write with fluency and power, but also write long, well-developed, shapely texts.

Look again at that sample piece for kindergarten included in Appendix C.

To day befor We had riyda groos Mrs. John red us a strorry a baowt frogs. We had to riet a baowt frogs. We haf a tadpol in the sciens sentr. It has 2 bac ligs and wen it has 2 frunt ligs its tal disuprs and it can not yet wen its moot is chajn. Then the scknn gets to little and the frogs pol off thrr scknn an thaa eyt it. Saum of the frogs bloo baubools. Frogs lad eggs that look like jele and the fish yet some but some hach to tadpoos. It gros bigr and bigr and bigr.

Kindergarten teachers debate whether this piece is a realistic goal for all kindergarten children and they are right to do so. But the point that matters is that the CCSS say clearly that in order for upper elementary teachers to bring children to standards, the teaching of writing needs to be a whole-school priority.

The standards acknowledge it will be hard for students to achieve the high level of craft that is expected of them if teachers haven't been moving them steadily along a progressing curriculum, extending their skills in each type of writing each year, and giving them clear expectations for their writing and feedback toward meeting those expectations. After all, in math, teachers ensure that students move up the grade levels with the essential skills that teachers agreed upon. That same focus on writing as content, as a set of skills, will move grade levels of students forward, rather

than simply those students who happened to get this teacher or that.

A child who wrote opinions in the primary grades, then moved to carefully constructed arguments in middle school, is going to be ready to embark on learning the skills needed to contextualize an argument, acknowledge and refute the counterargument, and analyze the research base and bias of sources.

Writing will need to be given its due, starting in kindergarten and continuing throughout the grades. Teachers will need to assess and teach writing, to track students' progress, and to plan interventions for those students who need extra help in writing. In short, writing will need to be treated just as math has been treated in the past. The standards give you a powerful voice in advocating for a writing curriculum and for time in the schedule for children to work on their writing.

Chapter 3

The Pathway along Which Young Writers Progress

WHETHER YOU ARE TEACHING someone to swim or to read, to play the oboe or to write, the learner needs to do the bulk of the work. What the teacher does from the front of the room cannot, alone, turn someone into a skilled swimmer or oboe player or writer; the learner needs to do it, and do it a lot.

Teaching writing begins with you sending children off to write and with children proceeding to show you what they can do. Once you end the first minilesson by saying those important words, "Off you go!" then you will want to watch closely to see what your children do. As you watch and talk with your children, you will learn what they understand about literacy. You observe, knowing that you will have a wide variety of writers in your classroom. In kindergarten, for example, there are children who write "squiggles and lollipops" and children who can, with only a little nudging and support, write pages full of readable sentences. It is your job to move each individual toward more and more proficiency.

> *"Teaching writing is not about waiting for children to grow on their own."*

Last November, a first-grade teacher said to me, "My first-graders are *still* just labeling. I don't know what to do." Puzzled, I asked what she meant. Was every child in her classroom writing only by labeling his or her drawings? She nodded, and repeated that her first-graders were just drawing pictures and recording labels on this or that picture. None were yet writing whole sentences under the pictures.

"Why *aren't* they writing sentences?" I asked, baffled.

She looked puzzled by the question, and said, "That's just it. I don't know why they don't do it. I keep waiting." Then she added, "I guess they aren't at that stage yet."

I didn't know her children and hesitated to say any blanket statement, but I couldn't help but think to myself that chances were good that her children weren't writing in sentences because they hadn't been coached to do so! Granted, even if she nudged one child after another to write sentences, paragraphs, even, progress wouldn't be instant or miraculous. But they'd at least be gaining the practice they needed to become more skilled.

Teaching writing is not about waiting for the children to grow on their own. Instead, teaching is all about knowing where a child is in a learning progression, knowing what comes next, recruiting the learner to be excited to tackle something new, demonstrating how to do that new thing, getting the child going on it with support, and then withdrawing the help and watching and celebrating as the child continues—sometimes shakily and with struggle at first. Meanwhile, as you watch, you anticipate the time soon when you'll teach the youngster how to take another step forward.

A LEARNING PATHWAY ALONG WHICH YOUNG WRITERS DEVELOP

Young children often progress in fairly predictable ways from scribbling (in lieu of writing) toward writing extended texts of all kinds. This means that even before you meet a new class of children, you can already anticipate a learning pathway along which those incoming children will probably travel. When you anticipate a learning pathway, you are more able to move each child along on that journey. Let's look at this pathway in detail.

Some children will draw and write as motor activities.

When you launch the kindergarten writing workshop (or the first-grade workshop if children did not have writing instruction in kindergarten), you will ask children to think of something important to them and then to draw and write about that on the page. Chances are good that most children will draw, and not even attempt to write, and that the drawings themselves will reveal a lot

to you. Some children do not try to make drawings that represent meaning. That is, for some children, drawing and writing are motor activities. During the writing workshop, these children are messing around with a pen. One child may fill the page with squiggles, another may make a small mark on one page after another, but either way, when you ask, "Could you tell me about your drawing?" the child will not have a lot to say about the meaning behind the marks. If you press, asking questions such as, "What's happening in your picture?" these children still won't reveal a meaning that their pictures carry. They will also probably not initiate any sort of writing.

How important it will be to help children in this category grasp the idea that texts carry messages, that pictures and words hold stories and information! Your first goal will be to help them approach the page with an intention to convey meaning. I might say to one of these children, "I like to write about the things I know about, don't you? What are some of the things at home that you know about?" If the child answers, "Cereal? I love cereal," I'll say, "Do you? What kind of cereal do you think is the best?" If I hear that the child loves Cheerios the best, I will say, "You need to put that here. Draw the bowl of Cheerios so people will know."

You won't always be present when children draw and write. When children in this category bring you texts that appear to be scribbles, you'll make a special point of conveying the expectation that the text *must* mean something. Pointing to a portion of the child's scrawl, you might ask, "What's this, over here?" Some children will probably invent a meaning in response to these questions, conjuring up the text's meaning long *after* they drew the nonrepresentational marks. The fact that the child attaches meaning to the marks on the page is a good thing, even if the child ends up creating a different meaning every time he goes to "read" those marks. Other children will have actually tried to convey meaning, and your interest will lead those youngsters to elaborate on the intended meaning by talking and drawing more. Some will have copied letters—correctly spelled words, even—from the environment. Either way, your goal will be to ensure that the child's drawings and marks represent meaning for the child. If youngsters are not encoding meaning into their drawings and their approximations of writing, helping them to do this will be your focus. Before long, they'll approach a page saying, "I'm making Cheerios: yum!" At that point, your conferring and small-group work can support sound-letter correspondence—and that work is described in the next section.

Some children will convey meaning in their drawings—but if they write at all, it's unclear what their marks say.

Some children will draw in ways that convey meaning. The meaning may not be readily clear to a reader, but if we ask, "Can you read me your writing?" the child has information to share or a story to tell. Although the content of the piece may be hard to grasp and may also be different every time the author returns to the page, these children nevertheless regard the writing workshop as a time for putting information and stories onto the page.

When you pull your chair alongside these writers, you will often find that the meaning on the page resides mostly in the drawing. The youngster may have labeled a few items in the drawing, perhaps with what appears to be random letters or letter-like forms. While your instinct might be to help the child correct any problematic letters and add more written text to the page, you would be wise to attend first to helping youngsters record their meanings accurately. One goal will be for these writers to be detailed, specific, and informative in their drawings.

"This is your family? Where is your mom?" I might say. Or, looking at the child's visual depiction of her mom, I might ask, "Where are her arms? No arms? She has to have arms, you silly, you know that!" I try to help children make their drawings more representational because I want to help them learn that "writing" involves conjuring up images of a subject and then working with diligence to record onto the page whatever is in their mind's eye. This is a basic premise behind all literacy. Learning to add detail to a drawing can be a precursor to learning to add detail to a written text. Learning to tell and draw more information (and to move from working on one page to working across the pages of a book) can happen first when the information is coded in drawings, and soon afterward when the information is conveyed through writing.

It's also crucial to convey from the start that a child's writing needs to make sense. I look carefully at the drawings and listen with great care to drafts, making sure I can actually follow the child's meaning enough to say back a coherent text. If I find a child's text confusing, I let the child know this and

recruit the child to rectify my confusion. "I'm confused. Is he flying? Oh, so he is standing on the grass. You might add that grass."

Because you will have encouraged your students to write as well as to draw, chances are good that children in this category will have some print on the page. You'll want to ask the child to read the message (even if you see enough diamonds and squiggles that you expect it can't be deciphered). If the youngster has trouble reading his or her writing, you can join into this effort. Don't give up easily on the job of discerning what has been said. If the child has written *HNE* beside the chimney on his picture of a house, say the letter *h*, listen for the dominant /ch/ sound at the end of the letter name, and with strong reliance on picture clues, perhaps you can successfully read *chimney*. It will be great if you can actually read some of the writing, but what is really essential is for the writer to see that you are intent on deciphering what he or she has written.

> *"If you keep your gaze fixed on the page and wait for the child to act, an extraordinary number of children will actually write."*

Of course, you will also ask the youngster to read the writing to you, directing the child to look at the picture and to point under the letters as he or she reads. If the child does read his or her print to you, or otherwise acts as if the writing says something, that's a cause for celebration.

There may be times when you ask the child to read his or her writing to you and it becomes apparent that the child has copied words from the environment rather than actually composing meaning. Sometimes the copied letters mean the child is trying to assume the identity of being a writer, but other times the copied letters reflect a child's anxiety and lack of understanding that the letters only matter when they convey meaning. Either way, in these instances, you will probably want to redirect the child to think about a topic he or she knows well and to draw that subject, then write labels to accompany the drawing. Your goal will be to help children learn that to write, you first must fill yourself up with content that is important to you and then reach for whatever means possible—drawing or writing—to convey that content.

If a child hasn't written at all, it is crucial to realize that this doesn't mean the child is hesitant or unable to write! Until you nudge the child a bit, it's impossible to draw any conclusions from an absence of print. And so you might ask these children to tell you what their page tells about and then say, "That is so cool! Why don't you write that?" Repeat the words the child said—perhaps the message was "I climbed the mountain"—and then say with confidence, "Write that." Say this as if you don't dream your instruction to write could possibly cause a problem. Point as you speak to a blank space on the page and keep your eyes fixed expectantly on that portion of the page. If the child doesn't immediately turn his or her attention to writing, you might go so far as to dictate, "I . . ." and again stare at and gesture toward the page as if certain the word you have just dictated will arrive there very soon.

This moment is always a revealing one! If you keep your gaze fixed on the page and wait for the child to act, the child will follow your gaze, and an extraordinary number of children will actually write. If a child says, "Is it *i*?" (or, conceivably, "Is it *e*?"), avoid confirming the child's every guess. "Put down whatever you hear," you'll say with a confirming tone. When the child has written something—anything—wait to see whether he or she will keep going. With time and continued expectation, many youngsters will carry on work—in which case, don't jump in to correct if it is not totally right! There is something very right about this work. On the other hand, if the child seems to either have given up after recording the one letter or to be stymied, coach the young writer to reread what he or she has written (reproducing the intended message whether that is, in fact, what is recorded on the page). Help in a way that brings forth the next word—*climbed*. Again, direct your gaze to the paper and watch with bated breath.

The child in this instance may produce random strings of letters (see the next discussion). Alternatively, the child may spell words by recording the dominant sounds (correctly or not), or the child may appeal for help. The help I'm apt to give is described under the section (on p. 23), "Some children label drawings but don't yet write readable sentences." Whatever the child does when nudged to write will be instructive.

Some children will write but seem to use random letters.

If a child writes but does so with what appear to be random letters, it's tempting to think, "This child doesn't know the first thing about writing." If you look again, however, you can see that such a child may have mastered some essential concepts—concepts such as left to right, top to bottom, front to back progression, and one-to-one correspondence.

You will also want to use your knowledge of invented spellings to look more closely for logic in the seemingly random spellings. For example, if a child has labeled a river this way—*YR*—that may seem totally random. But assume the child is using the letter name, not the sound linked to the initial letter (to the *y*) and assume, too, that the child is trying to write *water*. All of a sudden the spelling *YR* will seem like a logical early approximation. In the same way, *Dad* spelled with a *w* may seem like a random spelling until you say the letter name—not the sound—of *w*, and hear the very strong /d/ sound.

Sometimes, the best way to understand the logic that informs a child's spelling is to ask the child to continue writing while you watch. Channel the child to label whatever he or she has drawn while you sit watching. Then you will be able to see what it is the child wants to write, to hear how she goes about sounding out, isolating, and recording sounds, and to grasp the intelligence in her efforts and the roadblocks she encounters.

Of course, children need explicit instruction in phonics. During the writing workshop, you will want to teach students to listen for and record sounds, to rely on what they know, to think whether what they have written looks right, and to reread often as they write. You can certainly teach them some letter-sound correspondence. But you will also want to teach them to draw on the knowledge of letter-sound relationships that they develop during their word study time. Explicit study of phonics will power your writing workshop—and vice versa.

Some children know some letters and sounds but don't yet write them.

Although some children may enter school using lollipops, squiggles, and diamonds to represent oral language, most children actually come to school knowing most of their letters and sounds. Anne McGill Franzen addresses this in her book, *Kindergarten Literacy*. She writes, "According to the study [Early Childhood Longitudinal Study (ECLS-K)], two-thirds of entering kindergartners know their letters, almost a third can identify initial sounds, and about one-fifth can identify ending sounds!" (18). We strongly urge you, therefore, to not assume that your kindergartners must "begin at the very beginning." Instead, do a quick assessment of their knowledge of the alphabet and their sound-letter correspondence. You will probably be surprised to see that the days of children coming to school without knowing their ABCs are, for a majority of schools, a thing of the past.

Still, chances are good that some of your kindergartners, and perhaps even some first-graders, won't bring with them a strong command of the alphabetic principle. The good news is, that once in school, children will be immersed in work with the alphabet. They'll study their own and other children's names and talk about the labels in the classroom and in life. Holding up a stop sign, you'll say, "What might this sign say? The first letter is *s*, like in *Sam*." Children will read alphabet books and make them too. They'll sort and categorize letters. Within a few weeks of the opening of school, kindergarten children who came to school without knowledge of letters and sounds will know enough letters and sounds that they can join the rest of the class in labeling their drawings.

For a child to record letters to represent a word, the child needs to listen closely to the sounds within the word. Children don't usually arrive in kindergarten knowing that *dog* and *ship* each contain three sounds (the technical word for these speech sounds is *phonemes*). Many five-year-olds who are asked to tap out the sounds in *cat* will hear the initial and final sounds only. When children write, they are learning to hear and distinguish sounds in words (this is *phonemic awareness*). Children need not only to hear a sound but also to match that sound to a letter, recording it. "Let's say *me*," you might say to a child. "Say it with me." Together you'll say /mmmeee/ slowly. "What sound do you hear at the start of *me*?" you'll ask, adding, "Watch me, watch my mouth," and together you and the child again say /mmm/ and concentrate on the way your mouths feel as they make the sound. In this way, you'll help the child isolate the sound at the start of *me*, which is an important step. Pressing on, you might ask, "What letter makes /mmm/?" If the child suggests *any* letter, right or wrong, ask the child to record that letter.

The child may have no idea what the letter could be, in which case you will probably demonstrate how you think about this. Maybe you will repeat the /m/ sound and think to yourself, "Have I seen any words that start with /m/—/m/—*me*, /m/—*Mom*, /m/—*McDonald's*." You might continue, "It's like /m/—*Mike*," and point to a nearby *m* in the name chart. After deciding the /m/ sound can be written by the letter *m*, write an *m* and encourage the child to copy this letter onto his paper. "So let's read what you've written," you'll then say, recruiting the child to point under the letter and to read what he's written.

If the child required this much help with that first sound in the word *me*, you might not try for other letters within the word. The child will probably reread the one letter as if it says the entire word—*me*. Then you'll want to direct the child's attention to another part of the drawing and repeat the process of labeling something else and then another thing and another and another. The youngster can, of course, do that work without you—and will need to do so. Chances are good that at first the child will record only the initial or dominant consonant. Within a few days, however, this child will have written a score of labels, and you will certainly teach the child that words contain more than the first or dominant sound. If the child says a word slowly and tries to hear a second sound, that sound can be recorded, and then the child can reread what he or she has now written, saying the rest of the word. With instruction, children will hear more than one sound in words. (Granted, the sound that the child hears and the letter produced will not always be correct, but hopefully the choice will be logical.) Once labels include the dominant consonants in a word (*sn* for *sun*), making it possible for the child to reread what he or she has written and for someone else to read some of it as well, move the child toward writing stories and other texts that are carried by sentence captions under the drawing.

Some children label drawings but don't yet write readable sentences.

Just as it will be clear right away that some kindergartners will need encouragement to label their drawings, it will also be clear that with just a bit of encouragement and support, some children can write, "I ride my bike" using letters to convey at least the initial or dominant sound in the words: "I rd mi bk." For example, if many of your kindergarten children attended preschools of some sort, it is entirely likely that half of them will start the year able to write sentences, not just labels. It is important that your expectations aren't low, because low expectations can be toxic. Certainly, your first-graders should all be able to write sentences at the start of the year unless they were not given any opportunities to write in the preceding year, in which case expect the growth to happen within two weeks of the start of school.

The sign that a child can be graduated from labeling to writing sentences is, as I said earlier, that the child's labels contain enough of the dominant sounds that the child can read them (while also looking at the accompanying picture) and you can read them. If *sun* is spelled SN, or *bike*, BK or BC, then the child can be graduated to writing sentences.

At first, you will probably want to coach the child along. "What's that in your picture?" you ask, and when the child answers, you say, "You need to write that!" Then dictate the first word. "My . . ." If the child doesn't stretch the word out, listening for the first sound, coach her to do so. "Say it slowly, listening to the sounds."

Let her do that work. Don't do it yourself. If she says "Mmmmm-y," she is then apt to look up at you as if to ask, "Now what?" Say nothing. Look at the paper. Give her enough space that pressure mounts for her to do something. Don't worry when you see the learner struggling as this is exactly what you want to see—engaged hard work. You'll find that often, the youngster repeats the word, listens to the first sound, does this repeatedly, and after a bit, records it.

After the child has recorded one letter for a word that clearly contains several dominant sounds, wait to see if she initiates rereading and saying the rest of the word. If she doesn't, give just the barest of scaffolds. "Put your finger under what you've written, reread, and keep going."

Although this sort of scaffolding is necessary at first, it is equally necessary to pull back so that the child is nudged to continue as best she can. Of course, this will mean that the child bypasses a word or two, uses incorrect letters, and generally messes up. That's the price of independence. Your goal must be to withdraw your scaffold in such a way that the child continues voicing the next word, saying it slowly, and recording letters. Accept the child's approximations. If you jump in to be sure the child's approximations are correct, you keep the child in a dependent relationship to you, and the child will only write when you are on call.

Once a child has written one sentence, you are apt to feel exhausted. Your tendency will be to signal, "Great, now you are done." It is wise to remember instead that if a child can write one sentence, she can write two sentences. If the child can write a few sentences on one page, the child can easily move on to a second page. The hard work is evidence of growth—maintain it.

Some children write all-about books and stories (and other genres, too!).

If you teach first or second grade (and especially if your school supports writing), many children will enter the school year able to write sentences easily. Remember that every child deserves to start where he or she is as a writer *and to be challenged to go farther*.

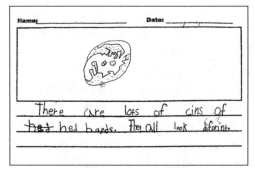

Page 1: There are lots of kinds of headbands. They all look different.

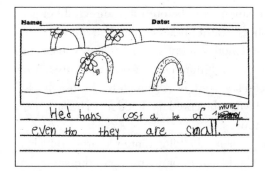
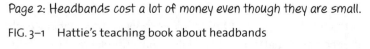

Page 2: Headbands cost a lot of money even though they are small.

FIG. 3–1 Hattie's teaching book about headbands

As I approached Hattie, I already had a sense of where in her writing she would need support. As the last unit came to a close, Hattie worked hard to add volume to her writing, despite the fact that she was writing for the duration of independent writing time.

"Hi, Hattie. Looks like you are hard at work. Is there anything that I can help you with today?"

Hattie looked up at me, knowingly. "I know I need to add more sentences," she started. "I just don't know how to do it." I read quickly through Hattie's teaching book about headbands.

"Hattie, you've got a goal that really makes sense for you. You are right that you need to add more information and ideas to your writing—your readers are going to want to learn so much more from you about headbands. So, when you want to add more to your writing, what do you do?" I knew my teaching needed to support her in using a strategy she could call on often, when working on any piece of writing, and that the point was absolutely not to help her have more content about headbands to add to her page.

At this point, I gave Hattie some wait time. This was not so easy to do, because I wanted to jump in and remind her of all of the strategies that she knew from all of the writing instruction that she had ever received. However, my goal is to help children set goals and then draw on their repertoire of strategies to meet those goals with independence.

"Well," Hattie started, "I could add more labels to my pictures."

"That's true! And then what?"

"I could . . . use those labels and pictures to help me add more?"

I confirmed Hattie's self-assessment, and before I left, directed her gaze toward a chart that could help her. "Hattie, that is great. You are right that whenever you want to add more and more sentences, one strategy you can use is that you can start by adding more and more labels to your pictures. After you do that," I continued, "you can add sentences to match all those labels." Wanting to make sure I extended what she could do, I added, "The labels are sort of like a way to plan the sentences."

Before I left, I helped Hattie get started adding more pictures and labels to her drawing. As she did this, she began to orally rehearse the sentences that she was going to add, as well.

On the fourth day of first grade, Omid's folder showed three papers, each featuring a rather conventional drawing and fairly conventional text. One read, "I like school. We riyt at school. We reed at school." Meanwhile, Omid had drawn a conventional picture of a butterfly, rainbow, and flower.

"What's your writing about?" I asked. Omid looked momentarily startled by the question but rose to the occasion and said in a staccato sentence that sounded like dictation, "The—uh—the—whatchamacallit—the—butterfly—loves—the—flower."

"Tell me about butterflies," I said, trying to bring Omid along.

"I never saw one," he answered. He was silent and I waited, waited, waited. Brightening up, Omid said, "But I saw a moth! I was trying to get it out of my house. I took a box and I put it very close to it and I pushed it in and I let it go in the air." He gestured to show me how the adventure had gone.

"Omid," I responded, "you've got to write that!" Then I said, "It'll probably be a long story. You are going to need a few pages!" I stapled three pages together. Then touching the first, I asked, "What will go on this page?" Omid wasn't sure. "Can you remember how your story about finding the moth went?" I asked and looked up into the sky as if I were mentally reaching to re-create the event. Omid joined me and said, as if dictating the story, "A moth was in my house and . . ."

"Okay, write that," I responded, pointing to the page. I dictated his words back to him, "A—moth—" Within fifteen minutes of writing, Omid had written the pages shown in Figure 3–2. Omid soon produced a coherent story that spanned several pages.

If a child is able to write a story, over time that child can learn to develop a setting, to show the internal as well as the external events, to write with literary language, to include dialogue, to decide which moments in the story are especially important and to stretch those out, and to incorporate techniques other writers have used.

BEGINNING WITH THE END IN MIND: REPRESENTATIVE EXAMPLES OF STUDENT WRITING

Lucille Clifton, the great American poet, once said to a colleague and me, "It's important to nurture your image of what's possible. We can only create what we can imagine." It's crucial that we teachers nurture our image of what's possible for young writers. Figures 3–3 and 3–4 are pieces of writing written by first-graders in the spring. These represent the horizon we need to reach toward as teachers of young writers. As you read these pieces, guard against the very human tendency to dismiss them by saying, "Those children are gifted." These pieces are well written but are not beyond the reach of many first-graders (let alone second-graders!), assuming those children are gifted with the opportunity to study with teachers whose expectations are high.

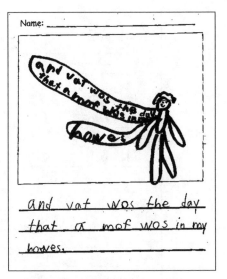

A moth was in my house. I got a box
and threw it out of my house.

FIG. 3–2 Omid starts on a coherent story.

The box had oil in it. The moth was
hurt a lot.

The moth fell down on the floor.

And that was the day that a moth was
in my house.

FIG. 3–3 Aiden's published book review

① Name: Annabel   Date: _____

One Day Mary was going to a hug aqwaryum. Mary was on a feld chrep. She was on the bus. Mary was ixitid. Mary was fiding a set.

② Name: _____   Date: _____

Mary's class went to see the sea onumols. Mary lookd at the pangwins. Then Mary lookd at the sels. Mary did not notis her class leve.

③ Name: _____   Date: _____

Then Mary trnd arawnd. Her class was not there. Mary was scard. Mary did not now wate to do. She was all alon.

④ Name: _____   Date: _____

Mary lookd and lookd she cood not find her class. Mary fawnd samone who wrkd there. "She said I am lost I can not find my class. enywav." The man said I will help you find your class littol girl. Mary was happy

⑤ Name: _____   Date: _____

The man took Mary all ovre the aqwaryum. Then Mary sol her class. "Mary said thats my class!" "Mary's techr said ware wre you" "Mary said I was lost". Mary thot I shud pay atenchun to my class next time

FIG. 3–4   Annabel's final fiction book

Chapter 4

Necessities of Writing Instruction

W HENEVER I WORK WITH EDUCATORS in a school, a school district, a city, or a country, I make a point of trying to learn about the vision that guides the approach to teaching writing. I ask, "What is the bill of rights that guides your work with your students as writers?" When people look quizzical, I rephrase my question. "When a child enters your school, what is the promise that you make to the child and his or her parents about the writing education that the child will receive?" I point out that chances are good that in math, the school essentially promises that child, "Whether or not your teacher likes math, you'll be taught math every day. You won't need to luck out and get a teacher who teaches math. And the course of study that you receive from one teacher won't be all that different from what you'll receive from another teacher."

Given that writing is one of those subjects that enables a learner to succeed in every other subject, the promise a school makes to youngsters as writers probably shouldn't be that different than the promise made to children as mathematicians. In this chapter, I share the essentials—the bottom line conditions, as we've come to call them—that school systems that provide effective writing instruction have in common.

Writing needs to be taught like any other basic skill, with explicit instruction and ample opportunity for practice. Almost every day, every K–5 child needs between fifty and sixty minutes for writing and writing instruction.

Although teachers must make decisions about their own teaching, no teacher can decide not to teach math nor can she decide, "I just teach math by simply tucking it into other subject areas." Channeling children to add up the number of pages they've read or to count the minutes until school is dismissed wouldn't suffice as a substitute for a math curriculum. Yet in some districts it is acceptable for teachers to say, "I just teach writing across the curriculum." Kids summarize their Magic Tree House book, for example, or answer questions about a film about sea life and these teachers call that writing instruction. But is it?

I often point out to administrators that when a teacher describes her writing instruction by saying, "We just weave writing across the curriculum," I tend to suggest that the teacher is probably saying, "I don't explicitly teach writing." Assigning children to write texts occasionally is not the same as providing them with a planned, coherent curriculum in writing.

Writing, like reading and math, is a skill that develops over time. Because of this, more and more schools are recognizing that children deserve writing to be a subject that is taught and studied just like reading or math. In thousands of schools writing is taught for an hour a day.

It is necessary that during writing time, children write for stretches of time. This means that for young children, the expectation is that they are writing something like a three- or five-page book a day—not writing a lead one day, an ending another day. Those pages might contain lots of labeled pictures for an early kindergartner or just a few lines for a first-grader, but the point is that the writer sustains work. Writing is a skill, like playing the trumpet or swimming or playing tennis or reading. Just as learners become skilled at playing an instrument or swimming or playing tennis or reading by doing those things, writing, too, is learned through practice. As my sons' tennis teacher says, "Success in tennis has an awful lot to do with the number of balls hit." Similarly, success in reading directly correlates with the number of hours spent reading. John Guthrie's study ("Teaching for Literacy Engagement" in *Journal of Literacy Research*, 2004) illustrates that fourth-graders who read at the second-grade level spend a half-hour a day reading, and fourth-graders who read at the eighth-grade level spend four and a half hours a day reading. Success in writing, like success in reading or tennis or swimming, directly relates to the amount of time a person spends doing that thing. This means that day after day, children need to write. They need to write for long stretches of time—for something like thirty or forty minutes of each day's writing workshop. And it means that volume and stamina matter.

Students date each day's writing, and all the writing stays in the students' folders until the unit of study culminates in a publishing party. This means that teachers, literacy coaches, and principals can look through students' writing folders and see the work that any student produced on Monday, Tuesday, Wednesday, and so forth.

Writers write, and a wonderful thing about writing is that it is immediately visible. This allows a school system to hold itself accountable for ensuring that every child has the opportunity and the responsibility to write every day.

"It has become increasingly clear that children's success in many disciplines is utterly reliant on their ability to write."

Children deserve to write for real, to write the kinds of texts that they see in the world— nonfiction chapter books, persuasive letters, stories, lab reports, reviews, poems—and to write for an audience of readers, not just for the teacher's red pen.

Donald Murray, the Pulitzer prize–winning writer who is widely regarded as the father of the writing process, recalls the piano lessons he was given as a child. The school system announced that anyone wanting to learn to play the piano should report to the cafeteria after school. Murray recalls his palpable excitement: at last, he was going to learn to make those beautiful melodies! In the cafeteria, children sat in rows, facing the front. Each child was given a cardboard keyboard and shown how to lay his or her hands on it so as to "play" notes. Children pressed their cardboard keyboards, but there was no music, no melody. Murray left and never returned.

Children deserve opportunities to write real writing; this means that instead of writing merely "pieces" and "assignments," children need to write in all the genres that exist in the world. A child should know that he or she is writing *something*—a nonfiction book, a book review, a persuasive letter, a lab report, a story—that writers write and readers read. The child needs to know, too, that others have written this same kind of thing and that one of the best ways to learn is to study the work that others have made, asking, "What did he do that I could try in my writing?"

Children not only deserve daily opportunities to write particular kinds of things—to write *something* that exists in the world—they also deserve opportunities to write for *someone*—for readers who will respond to what they have written. Otherwise, how will young writers learn that writing well involves aiming to create an effect? Craft and deliberate choice in writing are the result of thinking, as one writes, "They'll laugh at this part!" or "This will make them want to know all about it." To write with this sense of agency, children need to see readers respond to their writing. They need to share their writing with partners, to read it aloud to small groups, and to have people respond as readers do—laughing at the funny parts, gasping at the sad parts, leaning forward to learn more.

Giving children opportunities to write *something* (a letter, a speech) for *someone* (a younger class, a grandfather) makes it likely that writing will engage children and that they will feel as if the work they are doing is real, credible, and substantial. Children should not be asked to learn to play music on cardboard keyboards or to learn to write on ditto sheets.

Children need to be immersed in a listening and storytelling culture where their voices are valued and heard. Children will become better writing partners and better writers if they are encouraged to contribute their stories, opinions, thoughts, and ideas to a community of writers.

For children to want to put their voices and ideas onto the page, they need to be immersed in a listening culture. Too many children don't have opportunities at home to regale their parents with little narratives from their day, nor do they hear parents retelling the funny, sad, or important moments of their lives. Too often children are not teaching younger siblings how to do something or filling them in on all they know about a topic. It is crucial, then, that schools provide the opportunity for children to use language for a wide array of purposes.

One of the most important places to begin is to create, from the very start, a culture of storytelling.

In all of our classrooms, we have learned the importance of creating a culture where children's stories are valued and told. In some schools, teachers have decided to devote the first ten minutes of the day to create the culture of talk and listening. At the start of the year, this involves creating small circles of storytelling, and later, circles for teaching. When children talk to partners or small groups, they are teaching each other about topics they know well, instructing each other in how to do something, persuading others about opinions they champion.

In some of these classrooms, there are times—sometimes as often as one day a week—when this talking involves interested adults. That is, parents, grandparents, resource room teachers, and specialist teachers are all invited to come into the classroom to sit in small conversation clusters, listening to youngsters and helping them to elaborate, to say more, and to communicate in ways that others can follow. In other classrooms, these opportunities for talk occur during snack time. When the classroom brims with children's ideas, areas of expertise, stories, and opinions, then each child in turn seems to brim with ideas, areas of expertise, stories, and opinions. This is the perfect context for a writing workshop.

Writers write to put meaning onto the page. Children will especially invest themselves in their writing if they write about subjects that are important to them. The easiest way to support investment in writing is to teach children to choose their own topics most of the time.

Try this. Pick up a pen and write a few sentences about the sequence of actions you did just before picking up this book. Do it on paper or in your mind.

Now pause and try something different. Think about a moment in your life that for some reason really affected you. It might be the tiniest of moments, but it gave you a lump in your throat, it made your heart skip. The last time you saw someone. The time you realized you could actually do that thing you'd been longing to do. Write (or mentally think through) the story of that indelible moment. On the page (or just in your mind's eye), try to capture the essence of that bit of life.

Or try this. Think of a subject on which you are an expert. If you were to teach a class on a topic, what would it be? What if that course was done through writing. What would the first lesson be? How would you start it?

You will find that picking up your pen and writing a few sentences about the sequence of actions you just did—a kind of writing in which you throw out any old words—is absolutely unlike the other kind of writing—in which you reach for the precise words that will capture something important to you. For children to learn to write and to grow as writers, it is absolutely essential that they are invested in their writing and that they care about writing well. Children (indeed, all of us) are far more apt to be invested in writing if they are writing about subjects they know and care about and if they are writing for real, responsive readers.

It is hard to imagine an argument against letting children choose their own topics for most of the writing they do during the writing workshop. That is, when children are writing as part of a study of floating and sinking or weather, then of course, teachers will channel some of their writing to specific subtopics within those units. But if the youngsters are specifically working on their writing skills, they'll work the hardest if they are writing on subjects they have chosen. Although the craft, strategies, and qualities of good writing and the processes of writing vary depending on whether someone is writing an editorial or writing an information book (and therefore there are advantages to the teacher suggesting that the whole community work for a time within a particular shared genre), good writing does not vary based on whether the information book is teaching about the kinds of stones in a riverbed or the kinds of dogs in a dog show. Teachers can gather the entire class together and teach them about that kind of writing—for example, the importance of detail or of elaboration—knowing the instruction will be equally relevant to children who are engaged in writing about a wide array of different subjects.

The easiest way to help children love writing is to invite them to write about subjects they care about. When children have the opportunity and responsibility to choose their own subjects, they are not only much more apt to be invested in their writing, but they are also much more apt to be knowledgeable about their topics. In addition, they can learn what it means to rediscover subjects through the process of writing about them.

Children, early in their writing development, need to be taught phonemic awareness and phonics—the instruction that undergirds their language development and that supports and fosters their ability as writers.

The term *phonemic awareness* refers to the ability to blend sounds together to form spoken words and the ability to segment spoken words into their constituent sounds. Phonemic awareness is necessary for children to use their letter-sound knowledge as they read and write. Phonemic awareness is the beginning of literacy.

Most children develop phonemic awareness from language play and from opportunities to read and write. But some children don't have these opportunities, or have these opportunities but need more explicit help. Because we don't necessarily know which child will need what support, teachers are encouraged to plan for and teach a bit of phonemic awareness in kindergarten and first grade. Reading researchers who emphasize the importance of

phonemic awareness still suggest that kindergarten teachers spend a total of only twenty hours, spread across the year, teaching phonemic awareness (and less time in first grade). This works out to between five and seven minutes of phonemic awareness per day! That may be a small amount of time, but it is important to assess your children's developing phonemic awareness and to notice children who need more help with this because it is foundational. You can't spell sounds you can't hear.

The term *phonics* refers to sound-letter correspondences and to children's abilities to word solve as readers and as writers. Often, teachers structure the phonics component of their curriculum rather like a reading or a writing workshop, with an explicit minilesson followed by time for children to work independently, with partners or in small groups, with the teacher coaching them. In a phonics lesson, children are explicitly taught something, perhaps information about sound-letter correspondence, rhymes, spelling patterns, contractions, possessives, or the like. Then children use this explicit teaching in multilevel activities. For example, the teacher may teach a rhyme—perhaps *op*—and then children may work in partnerships to generate lists of words that contain that particular sound. Some lists will include *operation* and *helicopter*; others will be filled with one-syllable rhymes such as *mop*, *pop*, and *top*. The day's lesson ends with either a teaching share or another closure activity. Of course, on other days the instruction itself will be multilevel and delivered in differentiated groups.

When children are just learning about letter-sound connections, they need to know that when they are trying to spell a word, one of the first things to do is stretch the word out, breaking it into component sounds and recording the sounds they hear. Very soon, however, children need to rely on visual memory of the word and to use words they know to help with words they don't know how to spell. English words contain many letters that don't directly correspond to sounds, and children who struggle with spelling are often children who remain phonetic spellers. It's wise to have a consistent cross-grade whole-school approach to spelling and to organize this around the goal of helping all children develop the strategies that good spellers use. Never, ever say, "Spelling doesn't matter." That's not a wise message. Instead, say, "When you are writing and you don't know how to spell a word, try it; do your best and keep going."

Of course you hope that all of your wonderful teaching from phonics lessons and word study transfers seamlessly into the students' writing. Unfortunately the transfer of word study strategies and skills to independent writing can remain absent at times, because young children do not naturally see the interconnected hands of these two parts of their day. Often young students will need direct instruction to really see how to transfer their work from one to the other. They'll also need multiple opportunities, heavily scaffolded at first and then with a release of scaffolds as they become more accustomed to this work of transfer. This work might take the shape of interactive writing lessons that are geared toward demonstrating the use of word study concepts while writing a text, and then providing opportunities for students to try applying their word study concepts to the class writing. When interactive writing is a part of the writing workshop, several times a week, the children and teacher work together for ten or fifteen minutes to coauthor a very brief text on the easel. The class, meanwhile, writes the same text on white boards. This activity allows you to highlight features of written language and aspects of the writing process. Depending on what you decide to highlight, children may be reminded to use lowercase letters, to listen for and record blends, to leave spaces between words, to refer to the name chart as a resource, to rely on high-frequency words, to use end punctuation, and so forth. I suggest that interactive writing be kept quite distinct from the writing workshop and urge teachers to avoid using interactive writing to provide a story structure for children's own writing.

Children deserve to be explicitly taught how to write. Instruction matters— and this includes not just instruction in spelling and conventions but also in the qualities and strategies of good writing.

It is not enough to simply turn down the lights, turn on the music, and say to children, "Write." Nor is it okay to take anything that children produce and say, "You are an author!" It is not enough for children to have time each day to crank out genre-less, audience-less, model-less, revision-less journal entries. It is not enough for children to be assigned to do this or that writing task. Young writers are extremely vulnerable to instruction. Writing improves in a palpable, dramatic fashion when children are given explicit instruction and lots of time to write, clear goals, and powerful feedback.

For example, if a child is writing a how-to text or a science information book, that child may not discover on her own that it often helps to use numbered drawings to show readers what to do first, next, and after that. If the child has been shown the power of numbered drawings, however, she presumably can make use of this, and this one little bit of instruction can actually have an important payoff because it can help the youngster begin to order her writing as well as her drawing. There is no reason to wait and hope the youngsters will stumble on the power of numbered drawings. In the same way, the child may squish words together, not leaving spaces between them. Why wait to tell the child that actually, when you are sounding out a word and you come to a place where there are no more sounds, it is important to leave a little space there?

Then, too, a narrative becomes infinitely stronger if the characters talk. A very emergent writer can touch each of the people in her picture and say aloud what each person is saying. It is a small step ahead to add speech bubbles and to write what each character is saying—spelling as best this child can spell. Once a youngster has written a story ("I rode my bike") and added the speech bubble ("Oh no!"), it is a small step forward for that speech bubble to become dialogue.

I can walk into a classroom, look over children's writing, and know immediately whether children are being taught to write, because strong, clear instruction dramatically affects student writing.

When teachers explicitly teach the qualities, habits, and strategies of effective writing, that writing becomes better, and the improvement is evident within days and weeks, not just months.

One of the powerful things about writing instruction is that a good deal of it is multileveled. That is, say a writer is writing an information text, teaching all about the weather. If that writer has piled all that he or she knows onto a single page, chances are good that it will make an enormous difference to suggest the writer divide the topic into chapters, each addressing one subtopic. A child who labors to write a few sentences a day and a child who easily writes a few pages a day can benefit equally from that instruction. Both children, too, can look at a published information book to notice what the author has done that they could emulate. Actually, most strategies and qualities of good writing are multileveled. Some children will spell better than others, some will use more complex sentence structures than others, but many of the skills and strategies of skilled writing are within reach of every writer.

Children deserve the opportunity and instruction necessary for them to cycle through the writing process as they write: rehearsing, drafting, revising, editing, and publishing their writing.

The scientific method is widely regarded as so fundamental to science that children use it whether they are studying sinking and floating in kindergarten or friction and inertia in high school. In a similar way, the writing process is fundamental to all writing; therefore, it is important that children of every age receive frequent opportunities to rehearse, draft, revise, and edit their writing.

The important thing to realize is that teaching youngsters the process of writing is not the same as teaching them the names of the continents. The point is not for them to be able to parrot back the steps of writing well. Instead, the only reason that it is important for children to know the writing process is that when they aspire to write something, knowing the process is like knowing the recipe. For example, if a child is going to write a how-to book to teach someone how to play a game he has invented, his first concern should probably not be "What is my first sentence?" Instead, he'd do well to think first, "How does a how-to book go?" and "What kind of paper would be good to use?"

Of course, becoming at home with the process of writing is not unlike becoming at home with the process of doing long division or of solving word problems. It takes repeated practice. One learns and becomes more efficient over time. Things that once took a long time become quicker, more internalized, and more automatic.

This means that, most of the time, it is useful for children to have opportunities to plan for and rehearse writing, to flash-draft, and to reread their rough draft, thinking, "How can I make this even better?" Feedback from a reader can help a writer imagine ways to improve the draft. A writer will always write with the conventions that are easily under his control, but once a text is almost ready for readers, the writer will want to edit it, taking extra care to make the text more clear and more correct. Often the writer will use outside assistance—from a partner or a teacher—to edit.

> *"By studying the work of other authors, students develop a sense of what it is they are trying to make, and learn the traditions of that kind of text."*

Writers read. For children to write well, they need opportunities to read and to hear texts read, and to read as insiders, studying what other authors have done that they, too, could try.

Any effective writing curriculum acknowledges that it is important for writers to be immersed in powerful writing—literature and other kinds of texts. Children learn to write from being immersed in and affected by texts that other authors have written. They need the sounds and power of good literature and strong nonfiction texts to be in their bones. They need a sense for how an effective bit of persuasion can sway readers, for the way a poem can make a reader gasp and be still.

Children especially need opportunities to read as writers. Imagine that you were asked to write a foreword for this book. My hunch is that you'd do exactly as I did when Georgia Heard asked me to write my first foreword ever. I pulled books from my shelf and searched for forewords. I found half a dozen and read them ravenously. "How does a foreword really go?" I asked. Children, too, deserve the chance to read like writers. I'll never forget the first-grader who wrote in the foreword to his own book, "If you like my book, you get a prize. If you don't like it, you get mud."

By studying the work of other authors, students not only develop a sense of what it is they are trying to make, but also learn the traditions of that particular kind of text. Poets leave white space, how-to writers record steps, storytellers convey the passage of time. All writers care that the sound of their words matches the tone of their meaning. All writers care that they choose precisely right words. By studying texts that resemble those they are trying to make, children learn the tools of their trade.

Over the course of each day, teachers work with read-alouds several times for a range of purposes. On most days one of the read-alouds is an interactive read-aloud, with children talking in response to it, using accountable talk to develop ideas that are grounded in the text and in the conversation.

You might consider whether your classroom brims with the best of children's literature and with a reverence for literature. This is shown by the way books are featured around the room—as part of a science center, displayed along the chalk tray—and it is also evident in the care with which books are treated. Is there a hospital for damaged books? A special display for brand-new books? The library area, too, needs to be treated with respect. Ideally, children feel as if they are on a first-name basis with a few writers whom they know well.

Also, young children need experience doing reading work together with an experienced reader, in *shared reading*. During this time of the day, all eyes are on one shared text, and students can feel what it is like to read; they can get one step closer to being able to practice reading on their own. Buoyed by the support of the classroom reading community, children experience what it is to function like strong readers and, meanwhile, learn to integrate the skills and strategies that constitute reading as they experience a text together. During this time, you'll teach children to read class songs, big books, texts you've written together, and other writing that eventually becomes familiar to your students.

It is crucial that a child have at least thirty minutes a day to read as best he or she can. In kindergarten, much of the reading children do will be reading with training wheels of one sort of another. That is, children will reread texts they know from shared reading, they'll read very supportive texts with the help of a book introduction, or they'll reread rich storybooks they know well, relying more on the pictures and on their memory of the text. As this happens, you'll teach children to become conventional readers.

Children need clear goals and frequent feedback. They need to hear ways their writing is getting better and to know what their next steps might be.

Research by John Hattie (*Visible Learning*, 2008) and others has shown that to support learners' progress, it is important to encourage them to work toward crystal clear goals and to give them feedback that shows them what they are doing well and ways they are progressing, as well as letting them know next steps. This is especially true when the feedback is part of a whole system of learning that includes learners working toward goals that are ambitious and yet within grasp.

Effective feedback is not interchangeable with praise; it is not the same as instruction; it is not the same as a grade or score. While each of these may be a part of it, feedback is much more.

Effective feedback includes an understanding of what the learner has done and what the learner is trying to do or could do, a sort of renaming of the situation the learner finds herself in, including some of her history in this work. It is a particular response to exactly the work the learner has done. Effective feedback also includes an outside perspective—a reader's point of view, for example, or a teacher's point of view. Constructive feedback may include suggestions for the learner of strategies to try, obstacles to remove, or a baby steps to aim for toward the larger, more distant goal.

The "bottom line" conditions for effective writing instruction are, then:

- Writing needs to be taught like any other basic skill, with explicit instruction and ample opportunity for practice.

- Children deserve to write for real, to write the kinds of texts that they see in the world, and to write for an audience of readers.

- Children need to be immersed in a listening and storytelling culture where their voices are valued and heard.

- Writers write to put meaning onto the page. Children invest themselves in their writing when they choose topics that are important to them.

- Children need to be taught phonemic awareness and phonics—the instruction that undergirds their language development.

- Children deserve to be explicitly taught how to write.

- Children deserve the opportunity and instruction to cycle through the writing process.

- To write well, children need opportunities to read and to hear texts read, and to read as writers.

- Children need clear goals and frequent feedback.

Chapter 5

Provisioning a Writing Workshop

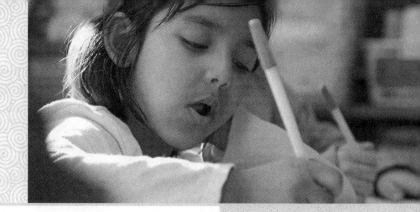

DECADES AGO, when I wrote the first edition of the now classic *The Art of Teaching Writing* (1994), I emphasized the importance of keeping workshops simple and predictable. Over all these years, this injunction continues to be an important one. Back then, I wrote:

> If the writing workshop is always changing, always haphazard, children remain pawns waiting for their teacher's agenda. For this reason and others, I think it is important for each day's workshop to have a clear, simple structure. Children should know what to expect. This allows them to carry on; it frees the teacher from choreographing activities and allows time for listening. How we structure the workshop is less important than that we structure it. (25–26)

> I used to think that in order to teach creative writing I needed to have a creative management system. I thought creative environments, by definition, were ever changing, complex, and stimulating. Every day my classroom was different: one day we wrote for ten minutes, another day, not at all; sometimes students exchanged papers, and other days they turned them in; sometimes they published their writing, sometimes they didn't. My classroom was a whirlwind, a kaleidoscope, and I felt very creative. Rightly so. My days were full of planning, scheming, experimenting, replanning. Meanwhile my children waited on my changing agendas. They could not develop their own rhythms and strategies because they were controlled by mine. They could not plan, because they never knew what tomorrow would hold. They could only wait.
>
> I have finally realized that the most creative environments in our society are not the kaleidoscopic environments in which everything is always changing and complex. They are, instead, the predictable and consistent ones: the scholar's library, the researcher's laboratory, the artist's studio. Each of these environments is deliberately kept predictable and simple because the work at hand and the changing interactions around that work are so unpredictable and complex. (12)

To teach writing, you need to establish an environment and structures that will last throughout every day of your teaching. The essential premise, one that undergirds any writing workshop, is this: the writing workshop needs to be simple and predictable enough that your youngsters can learn to carry on within it independently.

Because the work of writing is complex and varied, because students need to be able to follow their texts toward meaning, and because you need, above all, to be able to coach writers who are engaged in the ongoing work of writing, the writing workshop in most classrooms proceeds in a similar way through a similar schedule, using similar room arrangements and materials. Managing a writing workshop becomes immeasurably easier if youngsters are taught in similar ways through succeeding years, thus allowing them to grow accustomed to the systems and structures of workshop teaching. In this chapter, I describe, in depth, a workshop environment that is predictable and structured and that allows for student independence.

THE ENVIRONMENT FOR WRITING INSTRUCTION

Teaching writing does not require elaborate materials or special classroom arrangements. Teachers who teach in widely divergent ways can all offer children direct instruction in good writing. There are, however, a few room arrangements that especially support the teaching of writing, and you may want to consider arranging your classroom around the shared principles described in this section.

Room Arrangements

If I took you on a tour of any one of the thousands of schools where writing workshops flourish, you'd begin to notice the distinctive room arrangements even before we stopped into particular classrooms. Even as we walked along the corridor, peeking into classrooms, you would see that in most of these classrooms, there are spaces for students to gather, spaces for them to write, and spaces for writing tools and resources to be stored.

The Meeting Area: A Space for Gathering

In most workshop classrooms, one corner has been filled with a large carpet (nine by twelve feet or similar size), framed on several sides with bookcases, creating a library area that doubles as a meeting space. These carpets (and the communities that are created as the class gathers on them) are important

enough that when I recently met with a longtime TCRWP principal after she'd been promoted to the position of a New York City superintendent, she greeted me by saying, "Lucy, you'll be glad to know we put carpets into one thousand classrooms already." Usually, one corner of this carpet features a large chair that in some classrooms is referred to as "the author's chair," in honor of the times children sit there to read their work aloud (although actually the teacher sits in this chair the most). Always, teaching equipment will be nearby the chair, including an easel with chart paper, markers, and a fine-tipped pointer. Most teachers have a couple of charts going at all times, and the teaching point from each day's writing workshop is generally added onto one of the charts.

It's not only charts that need to be displayed, but also published texts and examples of student work and the teacher's demonstration texts. These are, of course, featured on bulletin boards, but it's also important for teachers to have a way to draw students' attention to particular aspects of texts during whole-class study. The Common Core State Standards' emphasis on close reading and evidenced-based instruction has made it all the more important for students to be able to make specific references to a text while discussing it. To help the class study texts closely, teachers try to have a document camera, an overhead projector, or a Smart Board nearby during minilessons, with a ready wall or screen on which to project enlarged texts. It is very inconvenient to move tables and chairs each time an overhead projector is needed, so you'll see that in most classrooms, a permanent lodging spot has been found for the equipment, one that doesn't require a lot of reshuffling to use it. For example, an overhead projector is often on a low table alongside the easel, angled toward the wall.

When children gather for minilessons or share sessions, they may sit in a clump or in rows on the carpet but, either way, drawn as closely as possible around the teacher. Most teachers assign children spots on the rug, moving the children who might otherwise sit on the fringes into positions that are front and center. Each child sits beside his or her long-term partner. Many teachers assign one child in each partnership to be Partner 1, the other, Partner 2, and often designate which is to take the lead during brief partner interactions within a minilesson.

Work Areas: A Space for Writing and Conferring

Although the meeting space is important in these classrooms, the most important thing is the rhythm of children sometimes pulling close around the teacher for a short stretch of clear, explicit instruction, followed by children dispersing to their work places, with the teacher now meeting with individuals and small groups as children write. That is, the rhythm in a writing classroom is not three minutes in which the teacher talks, elicits, and assigns and then five minutes in which students work, then three more minutes in which the teacher again talks and assigns, followed by another five minutes of "seat work." Instead, teachers teach explicitly for approximately ten minutes, and then students disperse to work on their writing for forty minutes.

It is critical, then, to think about the room arrangements that support students working for long stretches of time and that allow you to move among the students, conferring with them.

In many classrooms, children work at tables or at desks that have been clustered together to form table-like seating arrangements. (It is important that teachers check out the relative positions of chairs to writing surfaces to make sure that no student is writing at armpit level. Try this yourself, and you'll see it is extremely difficult to do!) During writing time, students often sit beside their writing partner. Partnerships generally last across a unit of study. Many teachers ask students to sit in "assigned writing spots" during writing workshop. These spots may be different from students' permanent seats, something that is possible because children own only the insides of desks, not the top surfaces, which are shared real estate. When children work at tables, not desks, the classrooms tend to provide each child with a cubby in lieu of a desk. Most classrooms also have a few desks that stand alone and are sometimes referred to as "private offices."

Sometimes teachers tell us they do not have space enough for a carpeted meeting area or for children to work at clusters of desks or at tables. Although this may sound strange to you, in more than a few classrooms, teachers create more space by foregoing some of their chairs. They usually do this by unscrewing the bottom half of the legs of a table or two, making the tables low enough that children can sit around them without chairs—an arrangement that creates space in an otherwise crowded classroom and also

allows children to sit in different ways at different times of the day. The low tables are either near the carpeted meeting area/library corner, or in a nook of the classroom, and children who work at these tables kneel or sit on their bottoms, sometimes with rug squares for luxury! In some classrooms, table lamps on these tables create a soft glow.

If you worry that when students are dispersed around the room, working at tables or in clusters of desks, they won't all be able to see whatever frontal teaching you do, there are a number of possible solutions. First, you can make a habit of convening students when you want to teach from the front of the room. In classrooms that explicitly teach students to make rapid transitions, it can take no more than three minutes for children to shift from sitting in their work areas to sitting in the meeting area, and of course, you are likely to get far better attention from students if they are pulled close to you. That option may not work for you, however, so another option is to teach students that when you are about to do some front-of-the-room instruction, the students who are sitting at tables far from the spot in which you stand know that they are expected to quickly shift their seating spot, coming to a place where they can see you. Others can remain in their seats.

Of course, you can teach writing well while maintaining a whole array of different room arrangements, and so although I recommend that you cluster desks into table-like formations and distribute them around the room, leaving maximum space between the tables, you can certainly make other choices. I do not, however, recommend that you line desks up into two or three long lines, making it almost impossible for you to ever come alongside a student, sitting shoulder to shoulder with that student. That position is an important one when teaching writing.

> "It is critical for the room arrangements to support students working for long stretches of time and allow you to move among the students, conferring with them."

The Writing Center

When considering room arrangements, you'll also want to think about whether you want your classroom to have a writing center—and if so, you'll want to think about the nature of such a place. I think it is a terrific idea to house resources in one nook and to designate that as a writing center. I could imagine you keeping a three-hole punch there, copies of touchstone texts, paper of different shapes and sizes, books on writing well, dictionaries, and the like. But it is unlikely that you'll want such a center to be a place where four or five students sit to write. Teachers who use writing centers as places to write tend to teach language arts by rotating students through various centers. This is often a way for the teacher to assign students various independent activities to keep them busy while the teacher leads a succession of reading groups. Writing, then, becomes a hands-off, laissez-faire activity. In my experience, students don't become much more skilled as writers without instruction.

Materials

When a school decides to spotlight the teaching of writing, the good news is that this doesn't require a whole new cycle of budgets. A teacher really doesn't need much to teach writing: paper, pens, storage containers. Other curricular initiatives often involve an enormous outlay of funds for a whole raft of new supplies, but reform in writing can proceed even if children sit on dirt floors and write on slate boards!

The interesting thing about materials for writing is that although writing instruction does not require fancy materials, the flip side of this is also true. Materials can make an exponential difference. There's hardly a writer on earth who doesn't have a fetish of some sort about the kind of pen or notebook or lined paper or font size or software program that allows his or her juices to flow. And I have never known a writer who doesn't use new tools as lures to help break down patterns of writing resistance.

When provisioning the classroom, you will certainly need to think about developing a system for managing children's actual papers and the materials they will need to write. One way to do this is by collecting student writing in folders and by making available writing toolboxes that include writing utensils and paper choice. In a well-run workshop classroom, teachers also develop, display, and reference classroom charts that the students then use to problem solve and to write with greater independence. You will also need to know what to do with student work upon publication and how to gather the necessary materials to share with parents during teacher conferences or open houses.

In the following sections, I outline systems that we've found to be effective for managing all the materials in a writing workshop classroom.

Setting Children Up with Writing Folders

In most K–2 writing classrooms, teachers find it helpful to give each child a writing folder and to use colored dots to code the folders so children who sit at the blue table, for example, have a blue box for their blue-dotted folders. When it is time for the writing workshop to begin, a table monitor brings the box of the appropriate color-dotted folders to the appropriate color table. Each child is taught to remove the piece he or she has been working on from his or her folder and then, to keep the workplace clear, to return the folder to its box, which is kept nearby for easy access.

All of the child's recent work within a unit is kept in the folder (and folders are emptied out after a unit, with the finished work either going home or going into cumulative folders). It is crucial that work is dated each day with that day's date stamp. This makes it very easy for a teacher to look through a child's folder and re-create what the child did in the writing workshop on Monday, Tuesday, Wednesday, and so on. Principals often sit down with writing folders as part of their supervision and want to see evidence of children's ongoing work. In many classrooms, children have a red dot on the left pocket inside their folders for finished (stopped) work and a green dot on the right pocket for continuing ("go" or in-progress) work. While children work in a particular unit—writing reviews, say—they write and revise many texts that pertain to that unit, so by the middle of a unit, the left side becomes full! Early in the year, kindergarteners may write two or three pieces a day; first-graders, two or three a week. As the year progresses, children tend to write fewer but longer and more substantial pieces and to spend more time revising and editing a piece.

Setting Children Up with Writing Utensils

In addition to providing children with a system for storing and cumulating work, you will want to think about the actual writing utensils. Teachers handle this differently. One decision is whether you want to influence the kind of writing utensil your students use and if so, what your recommendation might be, and the second decision relates to the question of whether writing utensils are privately or collectively owned. Obviously, there is no one right way to do any of this.

At least of at the start of the year, when you will want to move heaven and earth to lure children toward writing, and when supplies have not yet run low, many teachers try to make it possible for kindergarteners to write with sturdy marker pens, first-graders with thinner marker pens (although still the pens can't be ones that squish easily or they won't last long), and second-graders with pens. Because marker pens are hot items, that plan will only work if the markers are communally owned. Otherwise, one can imagine conflagrations arising over who the owner is of this or that marker. Of course, markers are expensive, and the supply often runs low a few months into the year, just when children are less apt to need this incentive to draw and write.

If you can't ever orchestrate things so that you can provide the class with markers, that's okay. Pens are a great alternative, and pencils are adequate, although we encourage you to avoid the thick red pencils that were once staples in kindergarten classrooms. (You try to write with them!) You will probably want to channel the class to alter their writing tools as the year progresses. For example, you might as well make the transition from markers to pens into a graduation of sorts. At some point, you can announce that because writers have grown so much, now instead of coloring during writing time, they will do the very professional work of sketching, and they'll do this so they can focus more on writing and double their expected volume.

Some teachers ask writers to choose their own pens, keeping a supply on hand in their backpacks and desks, but most teachers find it is more expedient to make writing utensils into shared property. You might supply them out of the school's budget, but more likely you'll ask each child to bring a box of pens into the classroom at the start of the year or, because costs decrease with quantity, you'll ask parents to chip in a few dollars toward a class kitty for pens. Of course, many supplies that are ordered at the start of the year will be withheld until they are needed.

In many classrooms, markers, pens, or pencils are stored in toolboxes, with as many toolboxes as there are tables (or other writing work areas). At the start of writing time, a table monitor from each table sets that table's toolbox at the center of the table. As soon as you have taught your students to revise (or reminded them they know how to do this), then the toolboxes will need to contain scissors and Scotch tape. As soon as you have taught writers to date their work, you'll want to include a date stamp. Many teachers keep a can of newly sharpened pencils in each toolbox and ask children to avoid sharpening pencils during the writing workshop. Instead, the entire set of pencils is sharpened as part of morning jobs. If a child breaks a pencil point, the child simply puts the broken pencil in the "to be sharpened" can. Most teachers suggest that if children write with pencils, it is best if they do not use erasers. After all, any teacher will want to see and admire children's drafts and revisions!

Setting Children Up with Paper

Of course, when provisioning a classroom with writing supplies, you will also want to think about the paper on which children will be writing. The system for dispersing paper is not crucial. What *is* crucial is that children need to be able to independently obtain more paper. In most of the classrooms I know best, there are one or two writing centers in the classroom, each containing a variety of paper for children to use as they need. Teachers tend to offer only a few paper choices at the start of the year; as the year progresses, they expand the number of options.

It is hard to emphasize enough that the kind of paper you give to your children absolutely affects writing that they do. Do *not* channel K–2 children to write in spiral notebooks all year long. For young children, the writing workshop is a time to make stuff, and that stuff has physical dimensions that matter. Constructing the physical artifact of a book, a letter, a recipe, a poem, a speech is a big deal. The cover, the sequence of pages, the final page, the back cover—all of that is a big deal. The paper on which a writer writes a how-to text needs to be altogether different than the paper on which a writer writers a story or a table of contents.

My very strong admonition against children writing in spiral notebooks may surprise those of you who are familiar with our ideas for supporting writers in the upper grades. You may ask, "Don't you encourage children to keep writer's notebooks?" The answer to that question is yes, starting in third grade, we encourage children to keep writer's notebooks. But there is a vast difference between the writer's notebooks some children in upper-grade classrooms keep and the journals we see in primary classrooms. Too often, these journals are containers for writing that has no genre and no audience (other than perhaps the teacher) and that is never revised, edited, or published. Because I want children to understand why people write and to draft and revise writing for readers, I vastly prefer inviting children to write all the kinds of writing they see in the world. As part and parcel of this, I encourage children to write on a variety of paper, but especially in small booklets that are easily revised.

The paper will be different based on the kind of text the writer is making—and based also on the writer's ability to write. You use paper to convey expectations. You assess what a child can do and channel that child to write on paper that provides the right mix of challenge and support. Over the course of a unit of study, the paper on which a child writes will probably change. Perhaps the pages in a first-grader's information chapter book are divided, with a place for a picture and half a dozen lines. Once that child has been writing up a storm for a few days, the teacher can say, "You are ready to graduate. I'm going to suggest that each of the remaining pages in your book be written on this paper," and then the teacher can produce paper with closer to fifteen lines on a page, and a smaller box for sketching. The teacher might produce a few adhesive mailing labels that the child could put where he or she needed to add diagrams or illustrations to the written text, suggesting that the writer could now use drawing to support rather than to plan for the writing. The point is that the paper needs to march just ahead of what students can do, so that it nudges them to write more, to grow more.

Creating and Displaying Classroom Charts

One of the big goals of your teaching will be to help your students develop a growing repertoire of skills and strategies that they learn to draw upon deliberately as they pursue their own important purposes. This means that it is a very big deal for you to make sure that your teaching has sticking power. In workshop classrooms, most teachers have found that they can use classroom charts to emphasize the fact that children should continually draw from their growing repertoire of strategies.

Some of the charts in a writing workshop are one-day charts. For example, in a unit of study on writing about reading, you might quickly jot some of the content that your second-graders noticed was conveyed by the illustrations rather than the written text in DiCamillo's Mercy Watson series. That chart is apt to remain for a day or two. Other charts, however, are anchor charts, and these tend to represent the accumulated teaching points from across a large swath of a unit. If a teacher teaches two information writing units—say, one at the start of the year in which children write about topics of personal interest and then one later in the year in which children write about a topic the class is studying in social studies or science—it would be expected that the anchor chart from the first information writing unit would resurface in the second. Sometimes anchor charts travel from one grade level to another, with teachers saying to second-graders, for example, "Last year you learned lots of ways to bring your stories to life." After referencing the chart that accompanied that teaching, the teacher might say, "Would you look at the story you just wrote and see how many of last year's techniques you remembered to use this year?" This, of course, could make way for the teacher saying, "This year, we'll add to the ways you already know for bringing a story to life."

Two of my colleagues have written an entire book dedicated to the wise use of classroom charts. In *Smarter Charts* (2012), by Martinelli and Mraz, you'll learn these and other tips for making charts that support instruction and encourage independence.

- Make charts with students, if not the whole chart, then a part so that children will remember the content.
- Make sure the heading names a big skill or goal so that children know the purpose of the chart.
- Use visuals (photos, icons, exemplars) to allow children to get a lot of information at a glance.
- Keep the charts current and up during the time children need them so they can access them at any point.
- Decide on the language of the chart ahead of time, considering vocabulary and student reading levels.
- Make the charts interactive. For example, have children add their names (on sticky notes) next to strategies tried, or have strategies written on sticky notes that can be borrowed as needed.

- Make charts clear and concise by using simple visuals, few colors, and easy-to-read print.
- Reread the charts often.
- Talk about charts often with the whole class, small groups, and partnerships.
- Periodically revise charts or retire them.

Usually classrooms also contain alphabetically organized word walls on which about forty high-frequency words are displayed (far fewer in kindergarten or at the start of any year), with the words often held in place with Velcro. In some classrooms, particular words on the word wall bear a star; these are words (such as *at*) that can beget zillions of other words. There are also lists containing words organized by sound (as in perhaps a list of *o* words).

Preparing for Publication

When units of study end (at approximately four- to six-week intervals throughout the year), each child selects one piece to improve and "fancy up" for publication. Publication always involves an authors' celebration, usually on the final day of a unit of study. These tend to become more elaborate as the school year progresses. The first authors' celebration might be as simple as parading around the room carrying finished pieces of writing that are then fastened to a "We Are Authors" bulletin board. Then the bulletin board might be toasted with juice and celebrated with cookies. Later in the year, a more elaborate authors' celebration might turn the classroom into a "museum" with children's work displayed on desks, full of Post-its that say "Ask me." The author sits near the work, ready to explain his or her strategies and decisions. Meanwhile visitors (including half the children at a time) visit the displays. During these celebrations, we would never ask the entire class to listen as each and every child reads a piece of writing aloud. Rather, children and visitors sit in one of five small groups, and in each group, children read aloud in sequence, with the listeners responding by chanting a refrain after each reading. Sometimes, they chime in on an adaptation of "Catch a falling star, put it in your pocket" and say, "Catch a fleeting moment, put it in your pocket, save it for a writing day." If published work can be word-processed by an adult, then a copy or two of each child's published piece

becomes an important part of the class library, available for readers. When this happens, children will often read their own and one another's writing during the reading workshop.

At the end of a unit, the pieces that are not published in any fancy way get divided up. At least one original piece is saved in the child's cumulative portfolio. Some may be given to particular readers. The remaining stash of work is usually sent home in a take-home folder (although there are times, including the first few months of the year, when the work is saved in school instead).

Meanwhile, we also encourage you to build in minor publications at the end of each bend in a unit. The anticipation of an audience is one of the reasons to invest oneself in writing. It isn't helpful for children to need to wait six weeks before they have that audience. We therefore try to build minor publication events into the infrastructure of a unit.

The particular system I describe here isn't essential. What *is* essential is that each child in the school needs to date and save each day's work so that children's work accumulates until the authors' celebration at the end of the unit. Often, a unit ends with students spending time revising work they have written throughout the unit, and then each of these writers needs the experience of his or her work reaching readers.

Collecting Student Work for Parent Meetings

It is also important that any system of clearing out the folders by sending work home doesn't start until teachers have both an opportunity to assess children's work and progress across the unit and to talk to the writer and his or her caregivers about this. If students' writing goes home in dribs and drabs without you having an opportunity to talk to parents about the ways that spelling will develop across the year, some parents may misunderstand your demanding approach to writing and spelling, thinking that the fact that students are expected to tackle even complex spellings on their own suggests lax rather than demanding expectations. The best system for teaching parents involves you accumulating evidence of growth and then, with evidence in hand, meeting with parents to explain your rigorous expectations. This means you will keep work in school until open house night or teacher-parent conferences. By then, any explanation you give about children's writing will be accompanied by convincing evidence of growth, and parents will grasp that incomplete spellings are a sign not of lax but of high standards.

Schedule

Time is the most precious commodity that any person has, and certainly it is a teacher's most precious resource. Each of you will need to design your schedule so that it is aligned to school, district, and sometimes state standards and expectations, as well as to your values and your children's interests and needs. The schedule will be somewhat different in kindergarten, first grade, and second grade. As children grow older, disciplines such as social studies, science, and math will be given more time, and choice will be given less time. Here are two possible daily schedules.

If other things must be squeezed into a day, another option is to cycle one component out of each day, so that subjects each occur four rather than five times a week.

Schedule 1

Prior to 8:30 Unpack, jobs

8:30–8:45 Morning meeting (songs, picture book, shared reading of the daily schedule, phonemic awareness, alphabet work with names)

8:45–9:45 Writing workshop (ten-minute minilesson, forty-minute work time punctuated by five-minute mid-workshop teaching, and ten-minute share)

9:45–10:15 Choice (dramatic play, blocks, alphabet center, art)

10:15–10:45 Phonics (including shared reading and interactive writing)

10:45–11:45 Reading workshop (minilesson that includes shared reading or a read-aloud; private reading; partner reading or centers— conferring, guided reading, and strategy lessons occur simultaneously)

11:45–12:30 Lunch and recess

12:30–1:00 Thematic studies (science/social studies, may include interactive writing, shared reading, reading aloud, or writing)

1:00–1:40 Special (dance/drama/science/art)

1:40–2:30 Math (includes calendar work)

2:30–3:00 Read-aloud and book talk

Schedule 2

Prior to 8:30 Unpack, jobs, sign in, talk

8:30–8:40 Morning meeting (as above)

8:40–9:40 Reading workshop (as above)

9:40–10:40 Thematic study/social studies/science

10:40–11:40 Writing workshop (as above)

11:40–12:10 Word study/spelling/phonics/vocabulary

12:10–12:50 Lunch and recess

12:50–1:50 Math

1:50–2:30 Special (science, art, music)

2:30–3:00 Read-aloud and book talk (rotating with gym)

SUMMARY

Writers don't need much: paper, a pen, a place to store yesterday's writing, a few wonderful published texts, a responsive reader of writing in process, crystal clear help in writing well, an anticipated audience—and time. Ideally, a writing classroom has a carpet on which to meet and an easel and a pad of chart paper around which to gather, but not much is called for! Because writers don't need much, it is entirely possible for a school system to provide writing workshops with all that is needed, and doing so is enormously important. I've watched writing workshops take hold within a year or two in every classroom up and down the corridors of a school, and when I try to discern the conditions that made it likely that teachers and children would embrace the writing workshop, one remarkably important feature was the fact that the provisions were available. Throughout the history of the human race, tools have made us smarter. The wheel, the stylus, the computer—these tools of the hand become habits of the mind, re-creating what it means to live and learn together. Teachers and school leaders, too, are wise to pay attention to the important work of provisioning writing workshops.

As described in more detail in the next chapter, managing children so they work with independence and rigor is a very big deal, and decisions you make about room arrangements and materials can play an important part. Even if your entire focus is on explicit teaching, bear in mind that until children can sustain work with some independence, you will not be free to teach. How *important* it is, then, for you to take seriously the challenge of managing and structuring your writing workshop.

Chapter 6

Management Systems

T O TEACH WRITING, you need to establish the structures and expectations that ensure that all students will work with engagement and tenacity at their own important writing projects. Otherwise, your entire attention needs to be on the effort to keep kids working—and you therefore aren't able to devote yourself to the all-important work of assessing, coaching, scaffolding, and teaching. Yet teaching young people to work with independence is no small feat!

You can start by recognizing that you need to give careful thought to how you will institute the systems that make it likely that your students will sustain rigorous work. When you plan your writing instruction, you will want to plan not only the words out of your mouth—the minilessons and the conferences that will convey content about good writing—but also the management structures and systems that make it possible for children to carry on as writers, working productively with independence and rigor. When workshops have simple and predictable structures and systems, teachers are freed from choreography and are able to teach.

THE IMPORTANCE OF STRUCTURES AND SYSTEMS

Why do so many people assume that classroom management is a concern to novice and struggling teachers but not to master teachers? Is there really a good teacher anywhere who doesn't think hard about methods for maximizing children's productivity, for inspiring the highest possible work ethic, and for holding every learner accountable to doing his or her best? I get frustrated when I hear some people say, with disdain, "She has trouble with classroom management."

Who doesn't have trouble with classroom management? How could it *not* be tricky to build an environment in which twenty or thirty youngsters each pursues his or her own important project as a writer, working within the confines of a small room, each needing his or her own mix of silence and collaboration, time and deadline, resources and one another?

Corporate management is considered an executive skill, and high-level executives are often coached in methods for maximizing productivity. Directors, managers, and executives attend seminars on developing systems of accountability, on providing feedback, and on organizing time, space, and personnel to maximize productivity. If the people working under your direction were grown-ups instead of children, the job of managing the workers would be regarded as highly demanding leadership work. But all too often in schools, classroom management is treated as something akin to doing the laundry. That's wrong.

As a classroom teacher, you absolutely need to give careful attention to methods of managing young children so that youngsters sustain high levels of purposeful work. You and your colleagues would be wise to assume from the start that classroom management will be a challenge and to give careful thought to instituting systems that channel children to do their best work.

LEARNING ABOUT STRUCTURES AND SYSTEMS THAT FREE TEACHERS FROM CHOREOGRAPHY SO THEY ARE ABLE TO TEACH

I recently visited the classroom of a first-year teacher. The writing workshop was about to begin. "Writers," Alexi said, "let's gather." As if on cue, Alexi's twenty-eight children gathered on the carpet, each sitting on top of a decorated writing folder, shoulder to shoulder with a long-term writing partner. Alexi took her place in "the author's chair" and began leading a ten-minute minilesson in which she named a strategy that writers often use that she wanted to teach, then demonstrated that strategy, gave her children a few minutes of guided practice with the strategy, and invited them to add that strategy to their repertoire. Soon, Alexi's children had dispersed to their writing spots, each hard at work on his or her own ongoing writing project. None of them required Alexi to come to their side and provide a personalized jump start.

As I watched all this, I marveled that Alexi, a novice teacher, was teaching in such efficient and effective ways. I remembered with a pang my first years as a teacher. "How did she get to be so good?" I wondered. But then I knew. Alexi is the teacher she is because although *she* is new to the profession, *her methods* are not new. Her methods have gone through hundreds of drafts and have been shaped by the legacy of scores of experienced teachers. This is how it should be.

The best way I know to learn classroom management strategies is to visit well-established writing workshops to study the infrastructure that underlies this kind of teaching. Writing workshops are structured in such predictable, consistent ways that the infrastructure of most workshops remains almost the same throughout the year and throughout a child's elementary school experience. This means that when you visit a writing workshop, you peek in on not only today's but also tomorrow's teaching. In this chapter, you and I will visit a few primary-level writing workshops when they're in full swing, and we'll pay special attention to the nitty-gritty of classroom management. I'll be at your side on this tour, commenting on what we see together. We'll pay special attention to the following lasting structures.

- Managing the minilesson: the beginning of each day's writing instruction
- Managing writing time: the heart and soul of the writing workshop
- Managing conferring: making one-to-one conferences and small-group instruction possible
- Managing the share session: workshop closure

MANAGING THE MINILESSON: THE BEGINNING OF EACH DAY'S WRITING INSTRUCTION
Convening the Class for the Minilesson

If you want to gather your children's attention, you'll want to rely upon a consistent signal that you use repeatedly to let children know that you need their fullest attention. You will presumably use that signal whether you want to talk to students about their writing, their reading, or their math. Many teachers I know have taken to singing out a chorus that goes, "Stop, look, and listen," whereupon children freeze, look at the teacher, and then sing back in a lovely echo, "Oh, yeah." In the quietness after this exchange, these teachers talk to the writers—quietly, not in a playground voice. Even more teachers signal for attention by calling out in a loud voice that parts the waters of the class, "Writers!" The teacher then does a 360-degree scan of the classroom, waiting for all eyes to be on her. Once she has everyone's fullest attention (and only then), she talks quietly, urgently, to all the writers.

You may question this detailed attention to how children move from one place to another, and there certainly will be teachers who prefer a more organic, easygoing approach. But for lots of teachers, especially those in crowded urban classrooms, transitions can be a source of delay and tension, and neither is advisable. A fiction writer once said, "The hardest part of writing fiction is getting characters from here to there," and this can be true for teaching as well.

Of course, if your real message is simply, "Let's meet," you may not need to go to great lengths to recruit everyone's fullest attention just to say that. You will still need a way to signal to writers that it is time to set their supplies out on their tables and to gather for a minilesson. Many teachers send a child from table to table, like a young Paul Revere, saying, "Writing time is coming, writing time is coming," and then teach children how to respond to that news, so that soon, once children hear that message, they automatically begin getting ready. As part of this, rather than trying to give new detailed instructions each day that itemize what children will need to bring to that day's minilesson, many teachers find it efficient to ask children to always bring their writing folders (which generally contain a marker, pencil, or pen slid into the pocket). If children sit on their folders, this keeps the materials out of the way of fiddling fingers, yet accessible when they are needed. At least at the start of the year, kindergartners are less apt to refer to their drafts during a minilesson, and so they often keep their folders in their writing spots, each child taking out the text he or she will work on that day and only *then* convening in the meeting area. The fact that these children have already laid out their writing tightens the transition between the minilesson and writing time and increases the likelihood that the minilesson carries over to children's work.

I find it striking that in classrooms in which the transitions are long and mired in tension, teachers often assume this is par for the course. They shrug and say, "What are you going to do?" as if they assume this is how writing workshops proceed in most classrooms. I've come to realize that many aspects of classroom management are shaped more by our teaching—and specifically our expectations—than by our children's developmental levels. When teachers make a point of teaching classroom management, thirty children can come and go quite seamlessly between the meeting area and their workspaces.

Establishing Long-Term Partnerships

When children gather on the carpet, they usually sit in assigned spots beside an assigned, long-term partner. Because your children will probably also have reading partners and those partners need to be able to read the same books (which consequently means they are ability-matched), you will probably make a special point of establishing writing partnerships that bring together children who are quite different from each other. Partnerships are comprised of writing peers who can help each other, but there is not one "teacher" partner and one "student" partner. Partnerships last *at least* the length of a unit of study and often longer (although you may have one or two youngsters who are especially trying as partners, and their partnerships may cycle more quickly than others).

When particular partnerships work well, you'll want to try to keep them in place over time. It's a great thing in life to find someone who can help you with your writing. If children are English language learners, the partnerships or maybe triads often contain a more and a less proficient speaker of English. For new arrivals, the partnerships may be language-based—two speakers of Urdu working together, for example.

Management During the Minilesson

The biggest challenge you will encounter when teaching a minilesson is to achieve that magical balance wherein your children are wide-awake, active participants—and yet their involvement does not turn a tight, economical bit of explicit instruction into a free-for-all, with chitchat and commentary and questions and free associations overwhelming lines of thought. Over the years, my colleagues and I have recommended different ways for you to walk this delicate balance, and frankly, you'll need to do some self-assessment and to decide on a plan that works for you and your students.

For years, we suggested that the best way to keep minilessons streamlined was for you to essentially convey to kids, "For ten minutes at the start of most writing workshops, I'll pull you together here on the carpet and I'll teach you a strategy that you can use to make your writing better. For most of the minilesson, this is my time to talk and your time to listen. I'll tell you what I want to teach and show you how to do it. Then you will have time to talk to a partner as you try what I've taught."

I still believe that many teachers would be wise to convey that message and to teach minilessons in which children are essentially seen and not heard until midway into the minilesson. I say this not because I think that is the perfect solution, but because I think the perfect solution is hard for mortal men (and women) to achieve. It is a real trick to allow for more active involvement while still modulating—limiting—that involvement.

But in this series, we go for the gold. We send a more nuanced message to youngsters. We say to youngsters, "I'll often channel you to talk, and then before you finish talking, I'll ask you to hold that thought and to listen up while I make a quick point. This means you need to watch my signals. There will be times to talk to the group, times to talk with a partner, times to talk to yourself silently, and times to be quiet."

That is, the minilessons in this series offer many more ways for students to be actively involved in the frontal teaching than there were in the early units of study books. I'll summarize the ways we involve students, equip you with some tips for modulating that involvement, and explain our decision making around this.

"The minilessons in this series offer many ways for students to be actively involved in the teaching, as well as teaching tips for modulating that involvement."

do it, so that they can come to insights. The challenge is to demonstrate something that the youngsters are also imagining themselves doing, so that as they watch us they notice how we do things differently—"better"—in ways that inform their practices. To recruit students to be engaged in our demonstration, we are apt to get them started trying to do the same thing that we will soon demonstrate. We start the demonstration with some guided practice. "How would you do this?" we ask, and get children started doing the work in their minds. Then—just when they are trying to do something—we say, "Watch me for a sec." This is what it means to demonstrate. For our performance to function as a demonstration, the learner needs to be on the cusp of doing the same thing and ready to notice how we do things differently. This requires a keen level of engagement by the learner, but again, this requires that we recruit kids to be on the edge of doing or performing something. Here, we take the lead, pointing out what we hope they notice in our demonstration.

- One of the goals of the first portion of a minilesson—the *connection*—is to involve students. More specifically, in the connection we often aim to help students recall the prior teaching that provides a context for today's teaching. We are apt, therefore, to ask a question such as, "What have you already learned about . . ." and to set children up to talk to their partner about this. Then we pause these conversations, saying, "I heard you saying . . ." using that as a way to highlight what children already know about a topic. This little activity is varied in a host of ways. We might read off a list of what we have taught, asking students to point to places in their drafts where they did that work—if they did. All of these little interludes for participation can be perceived, by children, as invitations to tell the whole class about whatever is on their minds, which then sidetracks the minilesson. So you'll want to ensure that you channel children to talk to each other early in the minilesson and not for half a dozen of them to take the floor, talking to the whole group in ways that belabor the start of the minilesson, and that those early talk interludes are very brief.

- During the *teaching* portion of a minilesson, we often teach by the method called "demonstration." We do something in front of the class so children can notice how we do that activity differently than they would probably

- During the *active engagement* portion of a minilesson, students' engagement of course increases. After demonstrating, the teacher says, "Your turn," or something to that effect, to signify that this is the active engagement section of the minilesson. Teachers set children up to be fully engaged during this time; usually, this means either to write-in-the-air or turn-and-talk with a partner. For example, if the minilesson taught that writers sometimes reread drafts, looking at action words and asking, "Is this the precise word I want to use?" the teacher would probably demonstrate by rereading a few sentences from a draft in front of the class, pausing at each action word, and musing aloud over whether it was the exact, precise word. Then she'd say to the class, "So let's try it." She might set the class up to continue rereading the text, saying, "If you find a place where I used a generic word instead of a precise one, would you write-in-the-air, showing your partner how you'd revise my draft?" thereby channeling children to say aloud the word they recommend substituting. Alternatively, the teacher could ask children to notice and then discuss in pairs the steps she went through to replace a generic term with a precise one: "What steps did you see me taking when I replaced *went* with *crept*? Turn and talk with your partner."

There are some messages you will want to send children about your expectations during the minilesson. Children need to know what to do if a partner is absent (join a nearby partnership, without asking you to problem solve). They need to know that during a minilesson, their job is to listen and look unless you signal for them to do something different—to talk to a partner, to write-in-the-air, to do some fast writing, to list across their fingers. They probably need to know that there will be times when you ask students just to say their thoughts or into the air, or into the group, but that generally, if you are talking, you don't expect them to call out. If that is a message you want to convey—and I suggest you probably do—then be careful not only to say that to your students but also to hold to it. That means that even if your very most amazing student calls out something brilliant during the minilesson, you'll want to signal, that actually, this is not a time for kids to say whatever thought crosses their mind. Of course, there will be times for children to talk in a minilesson—often to their partners—so you will want to show them how to make a fast transition from facing forward and listening to facing their partner and talking. They can't spend five minutes getting themselves off the starting block for a turn-and-talk (or a stop-and-jot), because the entire interval of that interlude usually lasts no more than three minutes!

All of these things are worth explicitly teaching. I've watched teachers practice the transition from listening to talking to a partner by saying, "What did you eat for breakfast this morning? Turn and talk," and then, after a minute, saying, "Back to me." If you take just a minute or two to coach into the behaviors you want and then remember to hold to those expectations later, you'll find this all pays off in giant ways.

MANAGING WRITING TIME: THE HEART AND SOUL OF THE WRITING WORKSHOP

While the minilesson sets the tone for the writing workshop and provides students with another teaching point to add to their repertoire of writing strategies, the main work of the day happens during writing time, when students are bent intently over their work, hands flying down the page, or are alternating between writing something, rereading it, drawing a line and trying that again, then again. It is during writing time that you are free to support, scaffold, and foster students' growth as writers in whatever ways seem most important for each individual writer. In this section, I'll provide an overview of the structures to consider so that your students are not distracted during writing time, including how to effectively send them off to write, the nature of their work, and how to balance collaborative work with silent writing time.

Sending Children Off to Work: The Transition from Minilesson to Work Time

The most important words of a writing workshop may be those that come at the end of a minilesson when you say, "Off you go." You will try to make it likely that children actually *do* "go off" and get started working. For example, if children lollygag on the way to their work spots, you absolutely will want to address this. "Writers, eyes up here," you can call, waiting for the class's full attention. Once the room is absolutely silent, you could continue. "Writing time is precious. I can't figure out why anyone would waste a minute of your precious writing time by walking like this," and then you imitate the meandering trip many of them take around the entire classroom, "instead of like this," and you walk with urgency to a writing spot. "You are wasting time when you could be *writing*!" The important thing is not that you use those exact words, of course, but that you act as if it is incomprehensible that children would waste their precious writing time.

You will probably have four or five standard ways to get children started on their writing at the end of a minilesson. Early in the year, especially, many teachers disperse children in clusters, and then while one cluster goes off to work, these teachers say to those who are still sitting on the carpet, "Let's watch and see if those writers *zoom* to their writing spots and get started right away!" Then, as the remaining class joins you in watching the children who are getting started on their work, you can speak in a stage whisper to the children who are gathered close to you, celebrating the writers who are being especially industrious. You might say, "Oh, look, Joy has her paper out and her folder put neatly away! She's rereading what she wrote yesterday! How industrious!" Of course, the other dispersing youngsters will hear you discussing them and they'll respond in all the expected ways.

Sometimes you will disperse children by saying, "If you are going to be doing [one kind of work] today, get going." Then you will say, "If you are going to be doing [another kind of writing work] today, get going." Finally you may say, "If you are not sure *what* to do today and need some help, stay here and I'll work with you," and soon you're leading a small group of children who've identified themselves as needing more direction.

Then again, you will sometimes say to youngsters, "Right now, reread your writing and decide what you need to do today while you sit here on the rug. Then get started doing that work! When I see that you are well launched, I'll send you off to your writing spot." That way, you can support the transition to writing, disperse children one at a time once they clearly have some momentum, and quickly spot and support children needing help.

It is easy to lose a tremendous amount of time in transitions. If you have a few standard ways to send children off from the meeting area to their work spots, that is a step in the right direction, but in general, you will want to pay attention to the seams of your day. For example, you will probably want it to be clear where children will sit during writing time. In most classes, children either have assigned places for the entire day or assigned writing spots. We generally find that it is helpful if a few children sit in different places during writing time than they do the rest of the day, leaving a bit more white space than usual at the tables and desks. For example, if one table is composed of six desks pushed together, it may be that two of those writers have writing spots in the math corner of the classroom, or on the far wall of the meeting area, where they write on clipboards. Obviously, those children need to be able to handle such work spots (without rolling around like tumble weeds), but it is helpful for anyone (and especially young children) not always to be expected to sit in the same chair, at the same desk, all day long. Then, too, if two children are missing from a table, that gives you a place to sit when you join that table (which I find far preferable to kneeling!). This also provides a margin of white space around the four children remaining at that table, making it more likely that they'll focus on their writing.

Once youngsters have moved from the meeting area to their work spots, many of them are prone to just sit there, waiting until you come around to

give each one a private jump start. If you see that pattern in your classroom, know it is common, and know, too, that you can alter the pattern. Otherwise, a lot of a child's work time ends up being consumed with waiting!

There are several things you can do to make it less likely that children transition to the start of work time by sitting there, waiting for you to come around. One thing you can do is let children know that the first thing writers do is to write their name on their papers (if this is a new piece of writing and their name therefore isn't already there) and to try to reread their writing if they are working on an ongoing piece. Once children are writing readable texts, these two tasks are fairly easy for writers to do. These two tasks, therefore, draw children toward more demanding work.

You will also probably want to do everything possible to make sure that students leave the minilesson with more clarity about the variety of possible things they can be doing that day. This means that you should notice if, at the end of a minilesson, half a dozen children swarm about looking for more explicit instructions. Take that as feedback on your teaching. Children are either confused about what they can be doing that day, or they haven't yet learned that they are expected to be able to make decisions and carry on with independence.

You will want to make sure that students are listening while you teach the minilesson and especially during the link at the end of the minilesson. Watch for signs of engagement. Let children know they can signal (a very overt shrug) if they are confused about something you are saying in the minilesson. If you have a paraprofessional or a student teacher, ask that adult to sit among the children during the minilesson and to model intense listening, drawing children into this sort of behavior. Ask that adult to especially signal "Listen up" to children needing this extra reminder. Just after the minilesson, the adult may ask the child who never seems to comprehend and recall directions to confirm (say back) what the child heard. "Good listening today," the adult can say. For a time, you may want to create an interval for children to retell your directions to partners.

It generally is helpful to start the writing workshop by spending a few minutes helping to settle all children into their work rather than immediately hunkering down with one child and then another. You might circulate through the room, using a quiet presence to communicate with a touch, a word, a smile, a glance, or a signal. Meanwhile, as you circulate, you can research for signs of trouble, either addressing them through a whole-class voiceover or noting them for future reference. In these ways, you avoid the syndrome of starting each day's writing time by rushing among kids, giving each one a personalized recap of the minilesson.

The Nature of Children's Work during the Writing Workshop

After children are settled into their writing nooks and have either resumed their ongoing work on a piece or begun a new piece, they are ready to get to work. Every day, children draw and write as best they can on topics of their own choice. During writing time, children generally choose a topic, plan a piece, write it, revise it, put it in the finished work section of their folders, and begin a new piece. That cycle might take half a day or three days—longer for more proficient writers who will work on more substantial pieces and have more rehearsal and revision strategies to draw upon.

The nature of the child's work will be determined by the unit. In one unit, children will write poems; in another, lab reports or persuasive letters and petitions or nonfiction chapter books. The teacher will often determine the genre and will sometimes ask writers to all work on a shared strategy. (For example, a teacher might say, "Today, among all the other work you are doing on your nonfiction books, will you take a few minutes to add headings, text boxes, glossaries, to at the least your most current chapter of your nonfiction book?") In the writing workshop, it would be rare for the teacher to determine the topic. (That is more apt to happen when writing is done across the curriculum.) That is, the minilesson is generally not a forum for the topic that children will be writing about that day; instead, the subject will almost always be chosen by the writer. Instead of assigning topics, the teacher teaches a skill or concept for the writer to keep in mind and to use as needed.

This means that a child's work is influenced by the day's minilesson, but children do not rely on the minilesson as the source of their work. One way to think of the role of a minilesson is to imagine your principal calling you and your fellow teachers together and reminding you of the importance of making anchor charts to accompany your teaching. This principal would then say to you, "Off you go," and you and your colleagues would head to your classrooms to continue the teaching you'd planned. You'd carry with you the reminder that it is wise to find opportunities in your teaching to make charts that cumulate all you've taught and remind children to draw on that repertoire. In this instance, the principal, like the teacher of a writing workshop, would hope that the instruction given would raise the level of your ongoing work, but the principal certainly doesn't expect that you will return to your classrooms and forego all plans to immediately spend a day on charts!

In one first-grade classroom, for example, on the day the teacher taught children to use carets to insert missing information, one child was writing a true story about finding an inchworm on her sock and another was writing a chronicle of how she'd asked the tooth fairy for five dollars, please, for a tooth that really hurt. Since the strategy of adding carets to insert missing information is broadly applicable to any day and any text, the teacher asked all her students to take a few minutes to reread their writing to make sure it made sense, using carets to insert missing words and information. The important thing to realize, however, is that this was far from the day's work! This was a five-minute diversion, and otherwise students were expected to have and pursue their own important writing agendas, drawing on all they'd learned from other days' minilessons.

Conversations in the Writing Workshop: Friendships, Partnerships, and Silent Writing Time

While very young children write, they talk companionably with each other—and to themselves. I sometimes say that I'm not sure if five-year-olds *can* think with their mouths closed! Most of the teachers I know best like young writers to work at tables rather than desks because this encourages the conversations that are vital to children's work. You'll want your youngsters to work side by side so they make running commentaries. These commentaries do a lot to make writing workshops into the richest sort of language workshop imaginable. An adult who sits close to a table full of writers will hear talk like this.

"My mom *feeds* baby mice. They are soooo cute!"
   "How do you spell *ee* like in happ*y*?"
   "Bear, bear, that's a bear. Hey—that's funny: bare-bear! Bare-bear. Bare naked bear. Bare bottom bear."

"Wait a minute. I got two *m*s. Mmmmm!"
"Know what my puppy does? She bites her tail!" "Mine bites *me*!"
"Help! My *y* is banging my *a* on the head. Oops! Look out!"

Of course, when you encourage children to work companionably alongside one another, talking quietly as they work, this can spiral into an environment in which no one gets any work done at all. You may decide to support quiet work for second-graders, with times and places for them to talk. And in general, you need ways to signal to children that they are too loud, too silly, too distracted. Many teachers use the same signal to quiet their classes that they use to pull their children together onto the carpet. "Writers," they say, in surprisingly dominant yet quiet ways. Your children need to know this is a signal that they *must* stop talking immediately *and look at you*. "I find that after I first teach this signal to children, I really need to use it a lot so they practice taking it seriously," Amanda Hartman, our associate director for primary literacy says. "For a week, I may use that signal two or three times in a day's writing workshop," she explains, adding, "And of course I use the same signal throughout the day, as it is always about consistency and follow-through." Amanda and others emphasize the importance of children focusing on them visually because visually cueing in fosters a mental cueing in. Once you have quieted the class, you can quietly, firmly, encourage them to use "two-inch" or "workshop" voices. A word of warning: at the start of the year, when you first institute this procedure, you may need to wait a very long time until everyone *is* silent and is looking right at you.

Earlier, I mentioned that if you teach second-graders, you may want to channel students to write more quietly, concentrating their talk into a few sanctioned talk times. The truth is that at some point midway through the year, some first-grade teachers also decide that their children are mature enough to benefit from silent writing time, punctuated with deliberately chosen intervals for talk. These teachers tend to institute whole-class "private writing times" and whole-class intervals for partnership talk.

"Many teachers like young writers to work at tables rather than desks to encourage the conversations that are vital to children's work."

Partnerships will exist long before a teacher suggests this division between silent writing times and partnership sharing times. As I described earlier, children sit beside their partners during minilessons and are often asked to turn and talk to their partner for a moment or two. Once children are accustomed to these scaffolded opportunities for talk, it is then a small step to have children meet in these same partnerships at the end of a writing workshop. Once the class is accustomed to having partnership interactions at the beginning and end of writing workshops, it's then a simple step to add silent work time punctuated by a partner sharing time in the middle of a writing workshop. At first the mid-workshop teaching points that support partner talk may need to involve children convening on the rug in the meeting area. "Writers, can you gather in your rug spots," the teacher may say halfway through a writing workshop, and then set children up to work with their partners. "It can help to tell someone the story you are writing. Right now, will Partner 2 tell Partner 1 your story? Tell it with details—the whole thing—and tell it in a way that gives your partner goose bumps."

In some rooms, these mid-workshop partnership shares become an expected structure. In these classrooms, the partner shares help children stay on task. Children work for as long as the class can sustain a focus (which tends to be between twenty and thirty minutes). When the room grows restless, the teacher interrupts children's writing to say quietly, "Writers, please meet with your writing partners." Some days, the teacher steers these five-minute intervals so the partnership conversations reinforce that day's minilesson; other days these conversations instead counterbalance the minilesson. When the teacher I described earlier gave her minilesson on rereading and using carets to insert missing words, her instructions during this interval were, "Today, will Partner 2 read your writing to Partner 1? Partner 2, remember to point under the words with your finger. Work together to make sure you can *both* read the text *and* be sure it makes sense. Fix it if you can. Use the caret if you need it. Then you can both get back to work." On that day, only Partner 2 shared his or her writing. The teaching partner, Partner 1, knew that another day, roles would change and he or she would have a turn to receive help.

MANAGING CONFERRING: MAKING ONE-TO-ONE CONFERENCES AND SMALL-GROUP INSTRUCTION POSSIBLE

When you confer and lead small groups, you will probably find it works best to move among children, talking with them at their work places, dotting the room with your presence. Although you won't come close to reaching every child every day, you can hold individual conferences with three children a day (four or five minutes per conference) and also lead several small groups (they don't require more time than a one-to-one conference), and this will allow you to be a presence in every section of the room. You make your presence matter more because, when talking with one child, you can encourage nearby children to listen in. For most of a conference, you'll probably want to deliberately ignore these listeners, looking intently into the face of the one child, which often spurs the listeners to eavesdrop all the more intently. Often, as your conference ends, you will want to generalize it to the others who've listened in. "Do any of the rest of you want to try that too?" you might ask. "Great! Do it! I can't wait to see." Here I describe conference management practices that help lead children to independence. For more on conferring and small groups, see Chapter 8.

Teach children never to interrupt when you are conferring.

Teach children that when you confer, you don't expect other children to interrupt the conference. Another child can come close and listen in, but he or she must wait until you've finished conferring to ask a question. If a child interrupts while you are conferring, you react in astonishment saying, "Don't you see that I'm conferring?"

Create systems of dealing with daily occurrences that don't require your intervention.

You create bottlenecks if you tell children (or inadvertently convey to children) that they must come to you for bathroom passes, permission to get more paper, help spelling unknown words, support in using the stapler, permission to declare their piece finished, and so on. If you notice a reliance on you, it helps to reflect on how you inadvertently created that reliance and think, also, whether it is necessary. You can avoid bottlenecks and circumvent a number of problems by teaching kids wise ways of handling tricky spots in the writing workshop. You can, for example, lead minilessons on using a stapler, what to do when you're done, and so forth.

Encourage children who feel they need help to leave their writing spot and follow you.

If a child, in the midst of writing, decides that he or she needs help, it generally works better if that child comes to you (waiting until you finish conferring or leading a small group) rather than staying in his or her seat. If the child waits for you while sitting in his or her seat, the child is apt to be disruptive to nearby writers because he or she is stymied. It's best to remove that youngster from the work spot and to keep the child under your sway until you can say, "How can I help?" Meanwhile, of course, the youngster can learn by listening in to the work you are doing with other writers.

Concentrate on teaching the writing process, not on making every child's piece the best it can be.

Sometimes bottlenecks get formed because a teacher institutes a policy that before a youngster can declare a piece of writing done, the writer needs the teacher's approval. Teachers will explain that without such a policy, children will file half-baked pieces away in the finished portion of their folder or will progress to new work without ever rereading and revising anything. It is right to be alarmed if children aren't revising; in particular, first-graders who have lived through a kindergarten writing workshop should have a far better command of the writing process than that! But if you try to save children from their mess-ups by tying them to you, by requiring that they check in with you at regular intervals, then you never really see the problem for what it is and get a chance to confront it. Children need to be able to go through the entirety of their own entire writing process, to show you and themselves what they do on their own, and to receive feedback on the decisions they made. For this to happen, you need to accept that they will do work that is less than perfect. You won't always be there to raise the level of their work, and that's okay. All you can hope is that they will do their five- or six-year-old best. Over time, your teaching will lift the level of what kids do easily and on their own. In the meantime, if you're hyperinvested in every piece of work being as good as you can make it be, you will be in for a lot of management trouble.

Create the expectation of a lot of writing work getting done each workshop time.

If children are expected to work hard and are held accountable for getting a lot done, the room will be more apt to have that wonderful "workshop hum." It is advisable, then, for you to think about how you can hold children accountable for getting a lot of work done during a writing workshop. If children don't get their math done during math time, they need to do it another time. Similarly, during writing time, there needs to be no option but to get a lot of writing done. If children aren't able to accomplish much work during class, you need to find other times for them to get the work done. Could a youngster who is repeatedly getting very little done be given extra time to write by channeling her toward writing during choice time? The child won't like it—but what are the consequences for writers who often produce nothing? The message needs to be clear that there is no option but to work hard and to write a lot.

Choosing Whom to Confer with or to Include in Small-Group Instruction

Although the context for your conferences will be created by the entire fabric of your teaching, conferring itself creates its own organizational challenges. For example, you will need to decide how you'll figure out which child to meet with next. Teachers develop their own idiosyncratic systems here. Some teachers enter a writing workshop with a little list in hand of writers they plan to see. The list may come from studying assessment charts or conferring/small-group records and noticing the children they haven't conferred with for a while, and from thinking about previous conferences that need follow-up. Alternatively, the list may come from thinking about or reading through children's work and deciding on both children who need help and children who could, with help, do exemplary work that might fuel the next minilesson, mid-workshop teaching, or share.

Personally, although I do enter a workshop with a list of the children with whom I hope to confer, I find it is important to be able to improvise based on the signals children give me. That is, if youngsters at one table seem unsettled,

I'm apt to confer with a child at that table, knowing that my presence can channel the entire group to work rather than socialize. Then, too, if one child is especially persistent about needing help, I generally assume he needs to be a priority—unless he is always at my elbow, in which case I'll respond differently.

I tell children that if they need my help, they should get out of their seats and follow me as I confer. I find this keeps the child who feels stymied from derailing his or her companions as well; in addition, the children learn from eavesdropping on conferences. The line that forms behind me also provides me with a very tangible reminder of how many children feel confused or stuck at any moment, and this keeps me on my toes. If I have six children in tow, then I'm not apt to overlook them for long.

Keep Conference Records

You will definitely want to record your conferences and small-group work, and it is important to develop a system for doing so that fits intimately into the rhythms of your own teaching. The important thing is that the writing about teaching that you do must help you teach better and help your students learn better. This writing needs to be attuned to your teaching, reflecting, and planning. You will probably go through a sequence of systems before settling, temporarily, on one. Five or six systems are especially common among the teachers with whom I work.

Some teachers keep a page on a clipboard that looks like a month-at-a-glance calendar but is, instead, the class-at-a-glance one. For the period of time this page represents (which tends to be two weeks), the teacher records the compliment and teaching point of any conference she holds. Sometimes, the grid has light lines dividing each child's square into several parallel slots, with alternate slots labeled either *c* or *tp*.

Alternatively, some teachers create a record-keeping sheet that culls some main goals from the learning progression for the type of writing they're teaching, and use that sheet to remind them of their goals for children's learning and to record their observations of children's work and their teaching.

Some teachers use learning progressions and unit plans to create a prewritten list of possible compliments or teaching points and carry these prewritten teaching points with them, checking off what the child is doing that merits a compliment, what they will teach, and what they recognize they *could* but won't be teaching.

Some teachers have notebooks divided into sections, one for each child, and record their conferences with each child that way. Others do a variation of this, recording the conferences on large sticky notes and later moving the note to the appropriate section of the notebook. Some teachers do an enlarged version: they post their conference notes on a wall-sized grid, which reminds every child what he or she has agreed to do—and serves as a very visible record of which children have and have not received this form of intense instruction. I like to record conferences in the student's writing folder, the logic being that this way when I return for another conference, I can look at both the conference notes and the work. At the same time, the child has a very tangible record of the agreed-on work and the pointers I have made, and this is alongside the child's own goals for himself or herself.

MANAGING THE SHARE SESSION: WORKSHOP CLOSURE

You will want to draw upon a handful of alternate ways that share time generally goes in your classroom and to induct children into those traditions right from the start. Share sessions fairly often involve partnership conversations, in addition to highlighting the work of one student that the rest of the class might use as a model and celebrating the strong writing work students have done that day. The teacher has a teaching point to make in the share, and she makes it while also helping children reflect on how one aspect of their work went.

When it is almost time for the class to stop work for the share session, a child might circle the room, letting children know it is time to finish up. Alternatively, you could intervene to announce, "Three more minutes." In any case, writers will need a bit of time to finish what they are writing. Then you'll decide whether for this share, you want to bring children to the meeting area, or whether you'll want to work with them while they are in their writing spots.

Either way, you'll probably begin the share by talking with children for a minute or two. You may plan to share one child's work, either by reading the

child's work aloud or by asking the child to do so. Then, typically, there is usually time for children to talk with their partners.

Children may alternatively hear the story of a child who tried a strategy the teacher recommended in that day's minilesson. "Nicole reread and, lo and behold, she, too, found that she had left something out, and look at what she did! By golly, Nicole used a caret to fix her story!" But if the share is literally a time to share, it will do so in ways that extend what children did as well. "Nicole found, however, that it was important not only to add information but to also subtract information. For example . . . You, too, might think about whether you could do this as well." You may recap by repeating something you overheard, but more likely, time will be running short so you'll simply sum up the day's work and make a transition to whatever you'll teach next.

"Children learn to write from the work they do, and establishing and managing a productive work environment is a critical aspect of good teaching."

Alternative Structures: Table Shares and Symphony Shares

You'll probably want another format for share sessions, and you can select the format that works the best for you. Some teachers like to use partnership shares when children are sharing work and use table shares when children are talking over their ways of solving a particular writing problem. That is, if your goal in the share is to encourage children to talk about how they are planning ways to end their stories, then you might suggest they have a table conversation about this. Some teachers use those table conversations as a prelude to a community meeting, which probably involves convening in the meeting area.

Alternatively, you may find that in your classroom, the ritual that I describe as a symphony share works well. In this ritual, you ask children to search for an instance when they did something well. For example, you may have taught children that when writing opinion pieces, they need to state their opinion and provide a reason for that opinion. You may have asked children to find a place in their text where they give a reason for their opinion. "When I tip my baton to you, would you read out one instance when you gave a reason for your opinion?" you could say, and then function like the conductor in a symphony, with one child after another reading a contribution.

Teachers I know have devised a few other alternative rituals for share sessions, and you should certainly see this as one more place where you can draw on your own imagination of what's possible.

WHEN THERE ARE MANAGEMENT TROUBLES

When children don't carry on productively in a writing workshop, it's important to take the time to diagnose the cause, realizing that sometimes, what appears as a classroom management problem is really an instructional problem. For example, a teacher and I may realize that the issue is not management, but inspiration. That is, it could be that you need to make greater efforts to convince children that writing is worth doing by creating an environment in which writing and writers are cherished. Is there enough responsiveness to writing—to children's writing and to that of published authors—that children want to put their stories and opinions and expertise onto the page and share them? Then, too, sometimes trouble that appears at first to be a management-related issue in fact grows out of the fact that children feel stymied, overwhelmed, and anxious. It is important to check that the expectations you convey (even inadvertently) are multilevel enough that every child feels as if he or she has work to do that is within that child's grasp. Do *all* children feel that they can do work you will honor? If children think that the writing their teachers value is beyond their reach, then they will whine, delay, and line up for assistance—and this will create bottlenecks because there will not be enough help to go around. In the end, if children don't regard writing as doable and worth doing, they will either act out or tune out.

But often, if children aren't carrying on productively within the writing workshop, the problem falls solidly within the province of classroom management. Usually in these classrooms, teachers are so busy rushing from one child to the next that they don't have time to stop and study the patterns in their classrooms. How easy it is for me to sympathize with these teachers, because often I, too, am so busy running, running, running that I do not stop to ask, "Where am I going?" What each of us needs to remember is that the answer can't lie in our running faster and faster. There's got to be a better way, but you can only discover that way if you give yourself time to observe, to think, and to secure help by anticipating and planning for classroom management.

Becoming an Observer of Your Own— and Others'—Classrooms

The first step requires that you become an observer of your own classroom. "Let's call kids to the meeting area and watch what it is that 95% of them do with automaticity when they are asked to gather for a minilesson. Let's see what they do without us saying anything," I say to teachers, recruiting them to join me as observers. "Let's watch also what they *don't* do." Later we watch again at the transition point between the meeting and work time. During the workshop, too, we watch for the trouble spots. What happens if we don't rescue matters? Is it after a certain length of time that things become frayed—or in a certain section of the room? For certain individuals?

Teachers of very young children, especially, often believe that the particular set of management problems they face are inevitable, that these issues exist because children are young and can't sustain work for long. Sometimes it seems that there are teachers who actually believe that long lines of needy children, constant interruptions, and only brief stretches of time on task are par for the course in the primary grades. What I find myself wanting to say is that such a mind-set is a self-fulfilling prophecy. It is important for teachers who feel as if classroom management problems are par for the course in K–2 writing workshops to visit other classrooms filled with children who are like your own.

I wish I could do that with you, my reader. I wish you and I could literally *time* the number of minutes it takes between the end of the minilesson and that lovely moment when a hush falls over the room and everyone is engaged. I'd want you to see that this transition needn't take more than three or four minutes. I'd want you to notice that many primary teachers *are* able to move among their children, that it is not pie in the sky to say that teachers hold five or six conferences or small groups a day. I'd want you to see that in many classrooms—yes, even in many of the crowded urban classrooms filled with learners who could be classified as at-risk—a teacher can confer and lead small groups during the whole workshop time without a single child interrupting to say, "Can I. . . . ?" I'd want you to see that classrooms containing twenty-eight kindergartners can sustain the actual writing part of a writing workshop for at least forty minutes.

Developing Systems and Structures to Anticipate and Respond to Classroom Management Problems before They Occur

Sometimes when there are management troubles in a room, I wonder if perhaps no one helped the teacher anticipate that these problems are inevitable and that the challenge is not to avoid these problems but instead to have systems and structures and techniques in mind for responding to them. No teacher need wait for the inevitable problem to arise before devising a solution to that problem. In the real time of your teaching, the challenges happen very fast, and you definitely don't have time to make considered responses. But in the mental movie of your anticipated teaching, you can stop the action and think, "What will I say when a child interrupts the minilesson to tell me about a broken pencil?"

Early this year, I watched a first-grade teacher gather her children on the carpet and begin to read aloud Bill Martin's quietly suspenseful story *The Ghost-Eye Tree* (1988). The room was hushed save for the teacher's voice and the voice of the story, which combined to cast a spell over the listeners,

drawing us in. Then, out of nowhere, big-eyed sweet Mario stuck his hand up. Holding his pencil toward his teacher, he said, "Look, it broke." The teacher, clearly unsettled by the interruption, whispered, "You can go sharpen it." Then, as the kids made a path for Mario (who nevertheless stepped on two or three hands), the teacher valiantly tried to resume reading.

Watching this generous and kind teacher, I knew she was in for trouble. I knew the next time she gathered her children for a read-aloud or for a minilesson, there'd be many more children whose pencil broke, who got a little blood under a fingernail, who had a stone inside a shoe. The problem is, Mario's interruption of the read-aloud isn't a one-time-only event. This moment will be repeated over and over, all day, every day. If we rehearse for our teaching to go wrong (as it will), we can be ready to respond to the inevitable curve balls.

In the end, then, although you must teach writing in responsive and child-centered ways, your ability to teach writing relies on your willingness to plan, to assess, and to give respectful attention to the job of classroom management. Children learn to write from the work they do; therefore, establishing and managing a productive work environment is a critical aspect of good teaching.

Chapter 7

Inside the Minilesson

J UST AS THE ART INSTRUCTOR pulls students together to learn a new glaze or a new way to mix paints, just as the football coach huddles his team to go over a new play, so too, teachers of writing pull children together for minilessons that open each day's writing workshop.

Minilessons are meant as intervals for explicit, brief instruction in skills and strategies that then become part of a writer's ongoing repertoire, to be drawn upon as needed. That is, every day in a writing workshop, you gather the learners and say, "I've been thinking about the work you are doing, and I want to give you just one tip, one technique that I think will help with challenges some of you are having or may have soon." Then you demonstrate the new technique and help children get a bit of assisted practice trying the technique in miniature

"The biggest challenge is learning not the content of minilessons but the methods."

ways, all within a ten-minute minilesson. After this, you send learners off to continue their important work, reminding them that they can draw on the strategy they learned that day as well as those they've learned on previous days. I've often said that the most important words of any workshop are the words that come at the end, when you say, "Off you go." In any workshop, it is important that the kids know how to do just that. They need to know that after the minilesson is over, they can resume the important work they were doing the day before, drawing on all they have learned all year long and especially over the recent weeks.

Usually, for a minilesson, children sit in the meeting area alongside a long-term partner, clustered as close to you as possible. This is not usually a time for children to sit in a circle, because conversations among the whole class are minimal. This is time instead for you to teach as efficiently and explicitly as possible. So, most teachers decide to ask their children to sit alongside a partner, at the teacher's feet, facing the teacher.

Although the teachers with whom I teach often worry over the content of their minilessons, the truth is that if you are teaching and learning alongside a classroom full of kids who are engaged in their own writing, you'll soon find that your mind will brim with ideas for minilessons. The biggest challenge is learning not the content of minilessons, but rather the methods.

THE ARCHITECTURE OF MINILESSONS

While the content of minilessons changes from day to day, the architecture of minilessons remains largely the same, and it remains consistent whether you are teaching reading or writing. The architecture of a minilesson (as we have taken to calling the design of a minilesson) is easy to learn and provides support for any minilesson you might ever write.

Minilessons are only ten minutes long, yet within those fleeting minutes there are four component parts.

- Connection
- Teaching
- Active Engagement
- Link

Connection

Minilessons begin with a connection. This is the "listen up" phase of a minilesson. Although this is a whole-class instruction, when taught well, a minilesson has an intimacy, and that tone is established in the connection. A connection might start like this.

- "Come close. I've been thinking and thinking about what the one most important tip I can give you might be, and it is this."
- "Writers, can I tell you a secret? I want to let you in on something that I do when I am writing, something I haven't told too many people about."
- "Last night, I couldn't sleep. I kept thinking about your writing and thinking, thinking, thinking about what I could say today that might

help. Suddenly, in the middle of the night, an idea came to me. I got out of bed and wrote it on a Post-it. You ready to hear my idea? This is it."

- "Last night, I was telling my family all about the cool stuff you've been doing. I told them. . . . Then as we talked about you, my sister said, 'Hey, Lucy, why don't you show them how to. . . .'"

In these and other ways, the connection of a minilesson signals to children that the teaching they're about to receive is important.

The connection has two parts. It begins with an effort to connect today's teaching to the ongoing work that children have been doing and to the children personally. You want children to know that today's teaching is nestled into their ongoing work. This first part of the minilesson, then, often refers to the anchor chart that lists what the class has been working on. For example, if a minilesson will teach a new way to revise, you might start the minilesson by recalling all the ways that the class already knows to revise. In the second part of the connection, you say, "Today I want to teach you . . ." and then you name the teaching point that crystallizes the most important lesson that the minilesson aims to teach.

At the end of the minilesson, the teaching point often becomes one new bullet on that anchor chart and the children are reminded that they can draw on the day's teaching point or the larger repertoire of related strategies. Children then leave the minilesson with not just a single strategy in hand, but rather with an expanded repertoire. Let's look at both parts of the connection, starting with the first part, where you try to connect today's teaching to the larger canvas of your teaching (and to the children, personally). Over the years, I've developed a few techniques that I tend to rely upon.

In the connection, I often try to recruit youngsters to recall the work that they have done prior to this lesson, work that provides the context for the lesson.

If I'm going to teach youngsters one new way to write persuasively, I'm apt to want to start the minilesson by helping children recall what they already know about persuasive writing. I might, for example, say to them, "You've learned so much about persuasive writing. I'm going to reread our anchor chart, and after I read an item, will you give a thumbs up if this is something that you do in your writing, and a thumbs down if this isn't something you've tried yet?" Then I read the list of techniques for writing persuasively that I hope children are already using and let them know that today, they'll have another opportunity to use all the techniques they've already learned—and they'll learn a new technique as well.

There are lots of ways to adapt this general idea. For example, I might say to children. "I was thinking today about all the ways you've already learned to write persuasively. Right now, will you list across your fingers three techniques you use often when you want to get readers to go along with your opinion?" Then after a moment for silent thought, I might say, "Turn and talk. What techniques for being persuasive have you already learned?" As children share their techniques, I probably scrawl what I hear them saying into a list and then pause the conversations to say, "I heard many of you saying these things . . . ," and then I would read the list.

There are more creative ways to accomplish essentially the same thing. "Writers, I've been thinking that for my birthday, I *really* want my sister to give me tickets to see *The Lion King*. I've been planning my conversation to her. I think it will go like this. 'I want them. I *really* want them. I *really, really, really* want them.' But then I realized that you all are good at persuading people, and I thought maybe you could give me some suggestions for how I could be more persuasive with my sister." Then, after harvesting a few suggestions, I could recap by listing the points they made about being persuasive. "So I'm hearing you say that effective persuasion . . . ," and in that way I could summarize a few techniques that the children already know about persuasive writing.

In the connection, I sometimes share tiny excerpts of student work and vignettes from working with students.

I'm always playing Johnny Appleseed as I teach, finding one youngster who does something that can nourish other writers' imaginings of what's possible. But I also keep a file of work from previous years and, frankly, from other people's classes. Children are interested in other children even if I need to preface my story by saying, "I'm going to tell you about something that one of last year's writers did." I save work that is funny, in particular, and also work

that represents problems many writers encounter. In one minilesson, I showed children a preface that a six-year-old wrote to his book, which said, "If you like my book you get a prize, if you don't like it, you get mud." I've always wanted to adopt his preface for my books as well! I used that to set up a minilesson about the importance of studying all the parts of a book, not just the body of a book. In another minilesson, I told about a child who tried to add excitement to his piece through exclamation marks—only he called them "excitement marks." The child explained to me, "You use one when you have a party and a whole line of them when a guy dies." That little vignette set the stage for me to teach youngsters other ways to add excitement to a draft. When I have wanted to teach children that some comparisons are more effective than others, I have told the story of a child who wanted to describe the sound that the waves make at his beloved beach. The child closed his eyes, re-created the sound in his imagination, and then told me what he planned to write, "The waves sound like a toilet being flushed." I used the story to explore connotations, suggesting the comparison didn't work all that well. In each of these examples, I use direct address to capture the exact words that the youngster said to me. I do not actually remember the exact words that were used, but minilessons are much better if we tell stories fairly well, and quoting the words that a person said and thought makes for a much more lively story.

Notice, that oftentimes, the work I share is not perfect work. In minilessons, I often want to talk to the class about an issue they're tackling, so it helps to tell a little story about a writer who faced similar challenges. If the story is being told as a cautionary tale about what not to do, I don't use the names and stories of children in that class but instead, children from other years or other classes.

In the connection, I sometimes tell a story that may at first seem to have nothing to do with writing, but that, in the end, becomes a metaphor for the lesson I need to teach.

I recently told the story to children about a phone call to my mother. She had all these problems that she told me about, and I listened and tried to help.

Then we were in the middle of talking when all of a sudden she said, "I'm going," and then bam! She hung up! I was holding a dead phone. I thought, "Where's my thank-you and good-bye?"

The children, listening, were entertained because they generally like to hear little true-life vignettes, but they thought the story was unrelated to writing until suddenly, in the teaching point, I made explicit the fact that readers, like people talking on the phone, expect a reasonable ending to the phone call. This, of course, leads right into teaching a variety of ways that people often end their pieces of writing.

The connection ends with a clear teaching point.

The teaching point is part of the connection and transitions students from the connection to the teaching portion of the minilesson. In the teaching point, you'll crystallize what it is you hope to teach in that day's minilesson. I work hard to make teaching points crystal clear and, when possible, memorable and worth remembering. Listen to a few teaching points.

- "I want to give you one tip writers use to write powerful letters. Writers might imagine the person is standing right beside them, and then they talk to the person—but on the page."

- "What I want to teach you today is that to write how-to steps that a reader can easily follow, writers picture themselves doing it—almost like they're watching video in slow motion, pausing often to say, 'What exact words describe what I just did?'"

- "Today I want to teach you that nonfiction writers use fancy words to teach others about a topic, and they are brave enough to write expert words, saying 'Oh well, I'll try my best' if they aren't sure how to spell the word. Writers sound out fancy words by listening to each syllable, sliding their finger across the page, and writing the sounds they hear."

- "Today I want to teach you that writers don't just tell a fact, a detail, they help readers to picture the fact, the detail, and to understand why it matters. One way they do that is by using comparisons."

- "Today I want to teach you that when writers have an opinion, they give *a couple of reasons*, not just one, and say details about each reason. They use phrases like 'for example' or 'I think that because' to bring in some details."

As you study those examples of teaching points and the scores of others in the series, you'll no doubt see that generally, an effective teaching point conveys:

- What writers often try to do—the goal
- Ways writers can go about doing that—the procedure

Very often, the teaching point starts with a phrase or a sentence about a goal that a writer might take on, and then the teaching point conveys the step-by-step procedure the writer might go through to accomplish that goal.

Notice, for example, the third teaching point above states, "Nonfiction writers use fancy words to teach others about a topic, and they are brave enough to write expert words, saying 'Oh well, I'll try my best' if they aren't sure how to spell the word." That's the goal. It's followed by the way to do this: "Writers sound out fancy words by listening to each syllable, sliding their finger across the page, and writing the sounds they hear." That's the strategy, told in a sequential step-by-step fashion. I wouldn't feel as if my teaching point earned its keep if it went like this: "Today I am going to teach you how to spell fancy words." Such a teaching point wouldn't be worth posting as a bullet on a chart or reiterating several times within the minilesson. That is, a teaching point doesn't simply name the terrain that the minilesson will cover. It actually crystallizes the most important lesson from the day.

Some Cautionary Advice about the Connection in a Minilesson

When working with teachers who are authoring their own minilessons, there are several predictable problems they encounter with the connections to these minilessons. One predictable problem is that some teachers have been taught that it is better to elicit information from children than to say anything to them in a straightforward way. The result is that some teachers begin the minilesson with a barrage of questions. "Class, yesterday we talked about . . .

what?" the teacher will ask. "And you were having trouble with . . . what?" she'll ask. You will notice in the connections we described that some of them do recruit bits of active engagement from students, but on the whole, the minilesson is only ten minutes long, and the most valuable place for active engagement is later in the minilesson, after you have shown youngsters how to do something and now give them a chance to try it out, with support. I suggest, therefore, that you avoid launching minilessons with questions, and above all, avoid asking known-answer questions in which you're looking for a particular answer. Children can't read your mind, so their answers will tend to take you off in different directions, turning a minilesson into a conversational swamp. You have the floor. Try to speak in interesting and clear ways.

The second problem is that teachers often have a difficult time grasping the huge difference between a minilesson and traditional teaching. These teachers see a teaching point as an assignment. You can hear this in the language they use. They'll say, "Today I want you to do . . ." or "Today you will. . . ." Those are the words of a whole-class assignment—laying out what you want all the students to do today—rather than the words of a teaching point. A teaching point lets writers know something that they can draw upon often, whenever they write.

If a teacher says, "Today I want you to add what the characters said to your story," or "Today I want you to add numbers and labels to your how-to drawing," those are assignments, not teaching points. Children may all do this activity, but it is unclear that another time, when in the same position, they will know how or when to self-initiate the strategy.

How different it is if you instead say this: "Today I want to teach you that whenever you are writing stories, it helps if you let the characters talk. A writer can do this by using talk bubbles or quotes to put the actual words that the character probably said onto the page." The difference is not just a matter of words. It's a difference of intent. In a minilesson, you must plan to teach writers something they can do repeatedly, perhaps today, and certainly for the rest of their lives.

Teaching

When planning the teaching, one of the first decisions to make is whether the instruction will rely upon a mentor text or not. Often one or two published texts are woven into a unit of study, with students returning to those texts

often to study new dimensions of them. Another option is to rely upon your own writing. Usually a teacher works his or her way through a piece of writing across the unit of study, in sync with the work members of the class are doing with their writing. The teacher may actually have completed the piece, but for the sake of instruction, she pretends not to have already written it, rewinding back to the start of the process, so that early in the unit, she might demonstrate how she generates a small list of possible topics and chooses one. Then, later, she might show how she gets started writing a first draft, and so on. Sometimes the class also has a text that they've been writing together, and that text, too, might be woven into the minilesson.

While thinking about whether one of those kinds of texts will be brought into the minilesson, you will also want to think about the method of instruction that you will use to teach. As far as I can figure out, only four main methods are available to any of us. We can teach people how to do something in the following ways.

- Demonstration
- Guided practice
- Explicitly telling and showing an example
- Inquiry

To help teachers grasp what it means to teach using these four methods, I often ask them to get into pairs, and I then ask one teacher to teach the other how to put on shoes, and to do this bit of instruction using a specific teaching method. (I don't discuss what those methods might be just yet. I simply suggest teachers do this teaching using a specific teaching method.) After two minutes, I stop the group and suggest that now, the second teacher in each partnership teach the first how to put on shoes, only this time I ask the teacher to use a different teaching method. We continue this until people have had four opportunities to teach the one lesson—how to put on your shoes—and then I ask teachers to list the methods they have used. As mentioned earlier, I have come to believe we have only four options: demonstration, guided practice, explanation with example, and inquiry.

Demonstration

The most common way to teach someone how to put on shoes is to begin by first taking off a shoe and proceeding to narrate the step-by-step process of putting the shoe on. That's the method of demonstration. The teacher may have done the work previously (I may already have had both my shoes tied securely to my feet when I started this lesson), but the teacher undoes that work (usually behind the scenes) to be able to redo the work publicly, this time naming the steps taken and tucking in little pointers. ("Sometimes you need to wiggle your foot from right to left a bit to get it actually into the shoe. Don't step down too hard on the heel of your shoe or it might fold in on you.")

Guided Practice

Second, we can teach in a way that walks our students through the process. Our shoes can stay securely on our feet, and our attention can shift to the learner who needs to start, shoeless. "Okay," we say. "Start by pointing your toe." Then we wait for the sock-footed learner to do that action. "That's it. Now stick that pointed toe right into the shoe, all the way to the far end of it." That's guided practice.

During guided practice, we guide children so that they have an instructive experience that they wouldn't have been able to have on their own. We engage children in the activity, and as they proceed, we use clear, efficient prompts to coach them along. We hope that once the minilesson is over, children will be able to do the same processes without requiring our guidance or support.

Explanation with Example

We could, instead, give a little lecture, complete with illustrations, to talk through the process of foot insertion into shoe. We could even use Power-Point to make a chart listing the four stages of foot insertion, with pictures to illustrate each stage. That's the method I call "explicitly telling and showing an example." The challenge when doing that sort of teaching is to make it informative and memorable. Decide on one name you will give for whatever you are teaching and use that one name four or five times in the minilesson. Think of what you are doing as giving children a little speech on a topic. Ask, "What content can I put in my speech? Will I share a few tips, tell an anecdote that ends up conveying a lesson, use a metaphor to teach a big idea?" You'll want to think over how to make your teaching memorable. Perhaps you'll use an anecdote or a metaphor, parallel construction, or a gesture that represents your content. In any case, this method of teaching requires more (not less) planning than the others.

If your explanation includes showing examples, you need to consider how you'll highlight the aspect that is germane. Often you can bring one aspect into relief by using a case of contrast.

Inquiry

Then again, we can simply say, "How do you think I got this shoe on my foot? Here's a shoe, here's a foot. Can you figure it out?" And that's inquiry. This method is most common when you want to engage youngsters in studying an example of good work, or when you want them to contrast effective and ineffective examples, generating descriptors of each. Sometimes this method actually combines the methods of demonstration and guided practice.

Planning a Demonstration: An Example

Each of these methods can be used to teach within a minilesson. To plan how the teaching component will go, I'm going to use the demonstration method as a model, because 80% of our reading and writing minilessons relies upon demonstration. Let's say this is my teaching point.

> Today I want to teach you that when you are hoping to convince someone of your opinion, it is important to not only *say* your opinion but also to add reasons. Usually the writer says his or her opinion, then adds, *because . . .* and puts in a reason.

To devise a minilesson that uses the demonstration method, it's important to guard against simply telling people about something you have already completed. Such a summary might start like this.

> Readers, I want to tell you that when I was writing my persuasive letter, arguing that there should be a fairer way to be sure all kids have a turn at the monkey bars, I realized I needed to add examples to support my opinion, so I added the word *because* and then wrote . . .

That's not teaching by demonstration. That's teaching by leaving your shoe on and simply looking back to explain (and perhaps showing an example). In contrast, if I want to demonstrate, the first thing I need to do is to take off my shoe, or to undo the writing work I have already done, so that I can "put my shoe on" (that is, write the passage) in front of the learners.

Before proceeding, then, let me share a few other tips about demonstration teaching.

Kids will learn more if you don't try to teach the entire process of writing within one minilesson.

In one minilesson, you do not want to show writers how you choose an issue that matters to you, decide on an audience for your efforts, figure out what you're arguing for, and also generate reasons to support that opinion. If the day's minilesson is designed to encourage writers to provide reasons to support their opinion, then the only writing work you will want to do is to generate reasons to support an opinion, adding those reasons onto an *already existing* persuasive letter. So to demonstrate only the new part of your thinking, you need to already have a persuasive letter that doesn't include any supportive reasons. So we are getting closer to designing an effective minilesson. The teaching component of the minilesson could start like this.

> Writers, you'll remember that yesterday we started this letter to the kids in Mr. Popper's class. In our letter, we wrote, "We are writing to ask you to please help us find a fairer way to be sure all kids have a turn on the monkey bars."

Then, of course, you could point out that the letter will be more persuasive if you include some reasons why this is important.

Kids will learn more if there is a predictable sequence of moves one makes in most teaching components.

Generally, in a minilesson—especially one where the teaching method is demonstration—the teacher starts by setting up the context for the minilesson. Often, this means showing writers that you have reached a certain spot in your writing process or have encountered some difficulty. Sometimes, it helps to just slow yourself down, taking time to think, to struggle, to say things like "Hmm . . ." That is, something prompts you to reach out for the strategy you will teach.

> I know we want to convince the kids to be fairer about the monkey bars. We're pretty sure we want to add some reasons. Hmm. What reasons could I give for why kids should be more fair. Hmm. It's not always easy to come up with reasons, is it? I have a trick that works for me. Let me show you.

Throughout the demonstration, it is helpful if you talk about the task as if the students are doing it with you, even though because this is teaching by demonstration, you do plan, in the end, to demonstrate in front of them. "I know *we* want to convince kids . . . to add some reasons . . ." You might go further by asking kids to join in the demonstration, like this.

> Try this. Try saying your opinion and then adding the word *because*. And sometimes reasons come to your mind. "We want to find a more fair way to play on the monkey bars because . . . A, and also because . . . B." Let's all see if we can come up with some reasons, okay? "We want to find a fairer way because . . ."

Then you model. You do the work that you want to show youngsters how to do. When doing that work, you will want to sometimes mess up in ways that you know youngsters will also mess up and then correct yourself, giving you more opportunities to teach. Modeling, we might say:

> "We want to find a fairer way because today it wasn't fair." No, wait, I have to remember to tell details. Let me try again. "We want to find a fairer way because today, Sari spent her whole recess waiting in line, and others kept cutting into line so she didn't even get one try on the monkey bars, and she spent her whole recess waiting."

Finally, you will want to explicitly name the steps you took, naming these in a way that is replicable to another day and another piece.

> Writers, did you see that to come up with reasons, I named our opinion, "We want to find a fairer way . . . ," and I added the word *because*, and somehow, just saying that over and over got reasons to come to mind.

Kids will learn more if they are trying to do, wanting to do, something that you demonstrate.

Brian Cambourne, the great Australian educator, once told me that people fly hang gliders over the field outside his office. On many days, he can look out his office window and see the people strapping themselves into harnesses and running pell-mell toward a cliff, whereupon they throw themselves over the cliff into the air. Brian pointed out that although he has watched this perhaps several hundred times, those hang gliders aren't functioning as mentors to him because never in a million years would he imagine himself doing what those people are doing. So he watches with detachment, not with the sort of identification that one brings to a demonstration. In the example above, there was a thin line between guiding students to do some work and the teacher demonstrating that work—and that thin line is characteristic of many demonstrations. Often the teacher recruits youngsters to join her in doing something, and then at some point, just when the kids are also engaged in the work, the teacher pulls ahead, performing the work for the youngsters in ways that highlight how she hopes they will all go about doing the work.

Active Engagement

After you teach something, you'll want to give children the opportunity to try what you've taught. Usually you'll do this by involving them in a bit of guided practice in which they do what you've taught while you interject lean, efficient prompts that scaffold them through the steps of what you want them to do or that lift the level of what they are doing. Setting this up takes some doing. Here are some options that are available to you, followed by potential problems to anticipate and solve.

Children continue the work on the next part of the demonstration text.

Sometimes, it works for children to help out with the next bit of work on the demonstration text. In the example described earlier, the teacher demonstrated how to go about adding one reason to support the opinion for fair use of the monkey bars, and certainly the most obvious active engagement would be to channel children to turn and talk, helping each other generate other reasons that could be added. As those children talk with each other, the teacher would probably want to do a voiceover, reminding them that their reasons should be detailed.

Children transfer what they have learned to do on another class text.

Imagine that the minilesson had instead been on titling a piece or ending a piece—on something that one does not do repeatedly in one piece of writing. In that instance, at the end of the demonstration, the work on that text would be done. There are generally a few options. First, often there is a class piece of writing as well as the teacher's own writing that could provide an opportunity for the youngsters to try their hand at work the teacher has just demonstrated.

Children transfer what they have learned to their own writing.

Another option is for the teacher to channel children to try this work on their own writing or on one piece of writing from within their partnership. For example, the teacher could say, "Would you take a minute and reread the opinion writing you wrote yesterday, and will you put a star at the place where you think you could add some reason?" Then, after a moment of work, the teacher might call out, "Partner 1, tell Partner 2 what you might add at that star. Help each other." Alternatively, the two members of a partnership could all along have looked at just one member's work. Then again, the teacher could have shared a piece of problematic writing with the class and recruited them all to pitch in, suggesting ways to improve that piece of writing. If the teacher is sharing problematic writing, she'll often create the text for the occasion and pretend it was written by some mystery student or a niece or nephew. "I'm wondering if you guys could help my nephew to do some of that same work. This is what he has written so far. Would you turn and talk? What tips do you have for what he might do next?"

Children act as researchers, naming what you have done in the demonstration.

Sometimes in the active engagement section of a minilesson, it is challenging to figure out a way for youngsters to practice what you've just taught quickly, and so you might devise an alternative way for the children to be actively involved. Typically, you'll devise a way for children to watch someone else (usually you) doing the work, and you'll ask them to function as researchers, articulating what they observed. You might say, "Tell your partner what you saw me doing that you could do too."

Children find and mark a place in their own writing where they could do the work of the demonstration.

Sometimes, when the teaching component of a minilesson has taught children something that writers do, you'll want to ask children to plan for how they'll do that in their own writing rather than actually doing that work within the minilesson. You might, for example, ask them to reread their writing and find a place where they could do that work. "Mark the place where you plan to do that with a planning sticky note that reminds you of your plans."

Predictable Problems during the Active Engagement

There are a few predictable problems you'll encounter during the active engagement phase of a minilesson. First, children can spend all their time on the logistics of this and never do the work. "You go first," one will say to her partner. "No, you," the other responds. "No, you." Or one child will push his paper toward the other child, and the back-and-forth will be, "You read it." "No, *you* read it." Teachers need to expect problems like these and teach students how to work well with partners. "Watch my partner and me," you'll say, roping in a student teacher so that you can reenact some of the horseplay you have seen kids doing with *their* partners. "Does this look like we're making smart use of our partner time?" Children will chorus, "Noooo." Then, for contrast, you can say, "*Now* watch my partner and me," and this time look your partner in the eyes, nod responsively as he or she talks, and so forth. You might make little asides as you do this, muttering, "Oh, what a great question! I love that question she asked!" or "Don't you love how she listens? I feel like she's really interested."

During this stage of a minilesson, the other great risk is that the *mini*lesson will become a *maxi*lesson and that children won't, therefore, have thirty or forty minutes to actually write. Short active engagements are hard to plan, but we must keep them short so students have time to write! If you wait until each child has completed the work you channeled them to do, or if you respond to all the confusions and questions that children have at that point, or if each child reports back to the whole group on what he or she has done, or if you also need to record each child's contributions on chart paper, this truly creates problems. There is no time left for the most important part of the workshop!

Link

Pulitzer prize–winning writer Donald Murray once told me that the single most important sentence in a paragraph is the last one. "This sentence needs to propel readers onward to the next paragraph," he said. "It needs to be not a closing, but a launch." I remember this advice when I reach the final bend in my minilessons. These last few sentences need to encapsulate the content of the minilesson in such a way that kids get their hands around that content and carry it with them as they head off from whole-class, teacher-led work into the whole of their writing lives.

The challenge when teaching is always to make a real difference—a challenge that is not for the faint of heart. It's a tall order indeed to believe that we can call children together into a huddle, take five or ten minutes to teach a technique, and they'll then actually add that technique to their repertoire, using it later and even again much later when the time is right. It is crucial to remind children that the particular teaching point of today is part of a larger repertoire of strategies that they will be drawing upon. This often means that in the link, you will reference an anchor chart (presumably the same one that was mentioned in the connection). When doing this, you'll want to remind children that the goal is not just to do the work of today's minilesson, but also to draw on what is now an even larger repertoire of strategies. You'll also want to remind them that, throughout their lives, writers always call upon a growing repertoire of strategies.

> *"Remind students that throughout their lives writers call on a growing repertoire of strategies."*

And so, you'll speak with great energy. "And so I'm hoping that today and every day," you'll say with great solemnity, knowing this repeating phrase may matter more than anything else in your teaching. "Whenever you are in this writing situation, you'll remember you can try . . ."

The link, of course, also needs to channel students to actually accomplish something concrete today, so this might be a time for brass tacks: what kind of paper, where that paper is accessible, what one might do first and next, and what is expected by when.

Then, there is the actual send-off. It might be that you channel those who will be doing one kind of work to get going. Then, after letting those children settle themselves down, you might channel those doing a second kind of work to get going. Then again, you might ask every writer to complete something on the rug and, when they have finished, to go back to their work spots.

THE ROLES WRITERS PLAY DURING A MINILESSON

I find it's helpful to teach children what *their* jobs will be in a minilesson. Explicitly. On more than one occasion, you'll say, "Today and every day in the minilesson, when I say, 'Writers, let's gather,' you'll get your writing folder and hurry here. You'll sit on your folders and you'll sit on your rug spot with your writing partner beside you. Then I'll talk to you for a few minutes. When I talk to you, you're going to really turn your brains onto high [you'll act this out] and *listen*, because I'm going to show you strategies you'll want to use in your writing. You'll do a lot of listening during that first part of the minilesson, and not a lot of talking." This introduces children to the connection and the teaching part of a minilesson.

You also want children to understand the third component, active engagement, and so you'll also say, "Then, after I show you something I hope will be helpful to you, you'll have time to try the strategy yourself, right here on the rug. Usually you'll turn to your partner and do some work together. Sometimes you'll be helping to think about a text the whole class is writing together. Then, after the minilesson, you'll go off to your writing spots, and you'll carry the strategies with you and use them as you write your own pieces on topics you choose." Your little speech doesn't mean children now deeply understand what is expected of them during minilessons, but it will help.

You may find yourself worrying over how you'll generate *the content* for your minilessons, and this will be the focus for much of this series. I'm convinced, however, that it's even more important for you to learn *the methods* of leading efficient, effective minilessons. When you study the craft of effective minilessons, this work can change your teaching not only in the writing workshop but also in every discipline, and it can improve not only your whole-class but also your small-group instruction.

THE TEXTS YOU USE WITHIN YOUR MINILESSONS

As I mentioned earlier, when we want children to do some work around a shared text, it's ideal to use a text you (or the class) has written about a shared

topic. This way, the piece is equally available to everyone. Perhaps the hamster escaped the day before. At home, you might write a scanty, underdeveloped story about the event and come to the minilesson asking for help. You'd have written a story that resembles ones children are apt to write (although, unless you are highlighting spelling, you'll usually spell correctly). You could begin the minilesson telling children that after you have written a story, you always reread it and think, "What did I leave out?" Then you could say, "So I'll reread a story I wrote last night. Could you join me in thinking, 'Is there more to add?'" Then you'll read aloud, as if you're a writer rereading and envisioning your story.

> We looked and looked. Then Robert saw some hamster food. We knew we were close. We found him behind the bookcase. We put him in the cage.

"I'm remembering that time, aren't you? Do you guys remember how Robert pointed to the food and said, 'He was here!'" Then you would say to the class, "Let's add that." As an aside, you might mention that writers do just what you are doing. They reread and sometimes remember the words a character *actually said* and then add those exact words. Then you'll either use a caret to insert the dialogue or, for younger children, draw a speech balloon over Robert's head, filling it with "He was here!" "Let's keep reading and see if there are any other places where we could make characters talk," you'll say next. Then you'd read "We found him behind the bookcase" with an intonation that suggests that you could *definitely* make a character talk at this crucial junction. "Tell your partner what we might have said when we saw him," you'll say, giving everyone a chance to try their hand at telling a partner how they'd add some dialogue into the whole-class text. Soon you will have elicited one person's suggestion and added it to the text. (I *don't* elicit a whole slew of suggestions.)

This episode shows how you can shift between teaching and active engagement and also shows how you can provide a great deal of scaffolding for children's active engagement. During the next day's minilesson, you might want to do almost the same minilesson with a different text, and this time you'd try to provide children with a bit less scaffolding. You might say, "I've really gotten excited about making my characters talk, and I've been rereading old pieces from long ago and thinking, 'Could I add talk to this one?' Sometimes I can't remember what people *really* said, so I just make up what they *might have said*. Let's try it together with this story. You remember, it was about when the toilet overflowed and came leaking into our room. I'm going to read *the whole story* without stopping—you can follow with your eyes—and then I'll ask you and your partner to find one place where you could make people talk. If you don't remember exactly what we said that day, you can think, 'What did we probably say?' Okay?" In the previous lesson, *I* was the one to locate a place that could contain added dialogue. In this minilesson, children are asked to locate a place for dialogue on their own.

Chapter 8

Differentiated Feedback

Conferring with Individuals and Small Groups

RESEARCH BY JOHN HATTIE (*Visible Learning*, 2008) and others shows that one of the methods of teaching that accelerates a learner's progress more than almost anything is the provision of feedback. If learners receive feedback that contains both acknowledgment of what that learner has begun to do that really works and suggestions for next steps toward an ambitious but accessible goal, then learners progress in dramatic ways. In writing instruction, one-to-one conferences and small-group instruction provide crucial opportunities for you to offer strong, individualized feedback and instruction.

Of course, providing feedback and instruction to youngsters requires that you have time to read student work and to talk individually or in small groups to learners. So the first challenge is not figuring out what to say in a conference or small group. It is figuring out how to scaffold and build student independence so that responsive teaching is even possible.

How is one-on-one conferring amidst a class even possible? How are small groups possible?

Whenever I gather teachers of primary children together to talk to them about the power of one-to-one conferences and small-group instruction, I find that a fair percentage of the teachers have trouble listening to a detailed description of what happens within a conference or a small group, because their minds are stuck on the questions, "How is any of that possible? How can you huddle with one child, or with four kids? What are the other children doing?" And if I explain that the others are carrying on writing with lots of independence, it is not unusual for a teacher to gesture me to her and quietly whisper, "My kids can't zip their coats without me. How could they possible *write* without me?"

These questions are absolutely critical to the entire enterprise of teaching writing. In fact, I can hardly imagine more important questions. The answers are complicated, and I will try to be as helpful and as clear as I can be. But I also want to suggest that you will benefit more from the upcoming section if you try to let yourself play the believing game.

I think it will help if you temporarily set aside the part of you that says, "No way. Not possible." Try reading the upcoming section realizing that in literally thousands and thousands of primary classrooms, kindergarten, first-, and second-grade writers can actually carry on as writers with enough independence that teachers find it relatively easy to conduct one-to-one conferences and small-group coaching sessions. And those classrooms *are* like yours. The writing workshop is thriving in large cities, in elite private schools, in rural hamlets, in international schools throughout the world, in public schools in Israel and Jordan, Mexico and Sweden—including, in some of those countries, schools that have fifty children in a classroom. The key question is *how* is this done, because there is nothing special in those schools or in those teachers' DNA.

Set children up to do work they can envision doing, want to do, and believe they can do.

Your children will be most apt to work with enough independence that you are free to teach if they are doing work (or trying to do work) that they can envision doing, want to do, and believe they can do. If your children all seem utterly dependent on you, perhaps you have set the bar too high, for now.

Early in the year, I think it is great to supply children with marker pens and with paper that contains plenty of space for drawing prior to writing. (I definitely suggest this for K–1 children and also feel like it is a reasonable option for second-grade children who haven't had experience in a writing workshop.) There are lots of reasons to support drawing as a form of rehearsal for writing, but one of them is that, frankly, it will keep your kids busy and engaged so that you can get around to them and do the teaching that is necessary to get them also writing up a storm. Nice marker pens do wonders for keeping kids working with independence! In the same way, provide your students with cool paper or tantalizing little books, stapled together, with just five sheets or so in a book so that they can start and finish a book often: presto! Giving children this exciting paper will mean that you'll be able to work with individuals and small groups while the others carry on.

Of course, the markers and the tantalizing booklets and the invitation to draw, as well as to write, have some limitations. First, assuming your goal is to accelerate students' progress in writing development, too much time drawing instead of writing won't necessarily be the best thing. Then, too, new materials lose their luster after a while (and become expensive).

But the larger point remains. If you want to figure out ways to manage the class so that you are freed to teach, you need to provide students with highly motivating, not-too-scary work for them to do. Engaging students in a sequence of steadily more challenging work is a critical part of any good curriculum, so those of you who rely on these units of study should be in good stead. But it is also important for you to always keep in mind that when children appear especially needy, it may be that you've just asked them to take a giant step forward, and they may be signaling to you that they need an interim step.

Provide clear expectations for the work that students can tackle with independence.

Make sure you are clear about what you expect children to do for themselves, as best they can, and don't give mixed signals. For example, if you want children to try spelling words with independence, then if a child asks you to spell for him or for her, you need to channel the youngster to do this on his or her own.

Sometimes a teacher will say to me, "I don't know what to do. My kids keep asking for help with spellings." My response is always, "That's because you keep giving them that help." If you consistently say to any child who asks for spelling help, "Your job is to spell that as best you can. Say the word to yourself, listen to the sounds, and spell it as best you can," then children won't find it all that rewarding to ask for spelling help—and they'll stop. If children are often lining up alongside you to ask, "How do you spell . . . ," then chances are good that you are intermittently reinforcing this. Instead, you will want to let the child know that either you always expect that he can tackle spellings on his own, or that there are certain predictable situations that lead you to provide the spelling.

But children are lining up not just for help with spellings, but also for help with all sorts of things—and again, chances are that you are reinforcing their reliance on you, or it wouldn't continue. If children come to you to ask for almost anything that is essential to their continued progress, you will want to think about whether that's actually working. Is your classroom organized so that you are the one to distribute paper? To provide access to the bathroom? The pencil sharpener? To a partner who'll listen to a draft? To grant permission to finish one text and start another? All of that can be outsourced, so that children know how to carry on with their work.

This may make you uneasy. How will you know if the draft has been done well enough that it can be pronounced done? How will you check on the amount of time children spend sharpening pencils if you're not in that loop? The answer, of course, is to actively teach children your expectations, to use the free time you gain to check on how youngsters have handled the responsibilities you've given them, and to teach in response to what you see. That is, you are still able to talk to children about work that has been declared finished and actually didn't match your expectations or about undue time at the pencil sharpener or in the bathroom. But your interactions will be designed to lift the level of this work not just this time, but in the future.

Actively teach children how to be problem solvers and how to self-manage.

When children come to you hoping for solutions to problems they could have resolved on their own, try to remember that although it may be easy to simply solve the problem, you are wiser to take the time to put yourself out of this job. Ask, "What do you think?" Then add, "So why don't you do that. And next time, I think you could solve a problem like this on your own." Alternatively, you might say, "I'm wondering if you need to come to me. I bet you can figure this out on your own." Your job in the conference will be to help the writer become self-reliant in the future.

This same work can be done in a small group. "I called you guys together because all of you are asking for similar help, so I wanted to talk to you as a group. You're all asking, 'Can I be done?' and I wanted to let you know the sorts of things you can do to answer that question for yourself. The first thing . . ."

As you do this teaching, whether in conferences or in small groups, remember that you help students become more self-reliant by reminding them to draw upon the classroom charts that contain all the tips they've been taught all year long.

Use strategy lessons when many children need the same conference.

Often you will pull a small group of writers together who might benefit from the same sort of help. "I pulled you together," you might say, "because all of

you seemed like you were having trouble getting started." We call this small-group instruction a *strategy lesson*, and I discuss these interactions in more detail later in this chapter.

THE ARCHITECTURE OF WRITING CONFERENCES

Most of us do not realize that there are times when our interactions with others follow a predictable structure, but this is nevertheless the case. In traditional classrooms, for example, the teacher will often ask a question, elicit a response from a student, and then evaluate that response. That is, the teacher asks, "What is the capital of New York?" The child responds, "Albany." The teacher assesses, saying, "Very good." This pattern of interaction doesn't often occur outside of classrooms and is not generally regarded as ideal. Usually, if a person asks, "What is the capital of New York State?" and learns that it is Albany, the response would be, "Thanks," not "Very good." Teachers who follow this question-response-evaluation pattern of interaction may not realize they are doing so. These teachers may think they are utterly changing their teaching when, for example, they work with new content (asking questions about Vermont, not New York, or about transportation, not government of the state) or when they ask questions that require paragraphs rather than simply a few short words of information. But the truth of the matter is that as long as the pattern of interaction in these teachers' teaching remains the same, the instruction itself will convey many of the same messages.

When a teacher confers with a writer, her interactions tend to follow a consistent pattern, one that teachers of writing have deliberately chosen and that reflects many beliefs about learning, teaching, and writing development. That is, although conferences *appear* to be warm, informal conversations, they are in fact highly principled teaching interactions, carefully designed to move writers along learning pathways. Here, I hope to elucidate the principles that guide me, and others, as we confer with young writers. Specifically, I'll discuss the architecture of writing conferences. That is, although writing conferences

> *"Although conferences appear to be warm, informal conversations, they are highly principled interactions designed to move writers along learning pathways."*

are intimate, infinitely varied conversations between a learner and a coach, there is a way that the structure of one writing conference is very similar to another. Afterward, I'll describe how the architecture of small-group work is very similar to that of a conference.

For any writing conference to work, the writer must first be engaged in writing work. That is, you must first organize and teach the whole class in such a way that each child is engaged in his or her own purposeful work as a writer. Then, you observe and coach in ways that either help the child do what he or she is trying to do or that direct the child to take on new (and perhaps more challenging) intentions. Either way, once you channel a writer to more challenging work, you usually need to briefly scaffold that new level of work. Then you pull back, encouraging the child to continue without relying on you as much.

This means that a writing conference almost always involves these four phases.

- **Research** what the child is intending to do and has done.
- **Decide** what to teach and how to teach it.
- **Teach** using one of four methods, each of which usually ends in guided practice.
- **Link** by extrapolating from today's work whatever it is that the writer will want to carry forward into tomorrow's work.

The predictability of these interactions makes them more powerful because writers can, in the end, use this same progression to confer with each other and with themselves. These Units of Study books are dotted with examples of conferences. As you read them you will see these principles in action.

The Research Phase

When I try to help teachers learn to confer well, or help them learn to improve their conferring, I focus on the importance of research, since that is the cornerstone of effective conferring. If you don't spend enough time trying to understand what the writer is doing and why, then what you decide to teach the student is often generic, perhaps just a recap of a minilesson. That is,

when a conference doesn't begin with a teacher taking into account what the child has done and is trying to do, then during the teaching phase of the conference, the teacher often just reiterates teaching that has already happened, unaffected by this particular student and his or her work. Your conferences can be among the greatest sources of originality and power in your teaching, but this can only happen if they are truly responsive. The vitality, originality, and specificity that characterize powerful conferences require that you, as a teacher, take in what the writer is understanding, doing, planning, and working to achieve.

Think about times when people have asked you questions such as, "How's it going?" or said things like, "Fill me in on what's been going on." My hunch is there are times when a question like, "How's it been going for you?" has led you to reflect on yourself, and your work, in ways that have created dawning insights about yourself and the work you have done so far, and there are other times when the same question has led you to stammer out a robotic or perfunctory answer: "Not that much has been happening, really." The difference in your response to the one question and the other probably has less to do with the words out of that person's mouth than with your sense of whether the person was really interested and sympathetic. When a person really listens, leaning in to hear more, nodding in ways that convey, "Say more," that intense and generous listening leads us to say more. We amplify, we illustrate, we elaborate, we connect. A good conference begins with deep listening.

Observe and interview to understand what the child is trying to do as a writer.

When you coach writers of any age, you need to first learn what the writer is already trying to do. You will grasp how important this initial phase of listening is if you realize that the conferences and small groups you hold with children about their writing are not unlike the interactions principals and staff developers have with you about your teaching. It's helpful if the person who coaches *you* first listens and observes to learn what you are already trying to do. Imagine, for example, that you had already spent months focusing on the strugglers in your classroom, and you decided now to nudge your strongest students to do better work. What if an administrator sat in on a few moments of your teaching and blithely told you that you mustn't focus on your strong students at the expense of your strugglers!

Of course, the administrator wouldn't have made that suggestion to you had he or she prefaced the visit by asking, "What have you been working on?" and, "How's it been going?" and even, "So can I watch that?" When supervision begins with listening, with learning about your goals, then the coach can either help you reach goals you have set for yourself or the coach can call to question the goals. ("I can see you have been working on X, but I want to urge you to work also [or instead] on Y.") When you think about what you'd want from someone who was observing and coaching your teaching, you quickly arrive at a list of dos and don'ts that pertain also to conferences and small-group work with young writers.

Because it is crucial to begin a conference by understanding what the writer has already been doing, you'll usually begin by watching—even just as you approach a writer or as a you scan a table, determining which youngsters you want to talk with. Make a point of noticing the writer's all-important engagement in his writing. Glance at the page, at the writer's work spot, trying to glean anything at all that can help you begin to understand the child's process as a writer. The research phase, then, begins with a teacher observing, interviewing, and sometimes reading the student's work to understand what the student is intending to do as a writer.

Help the child articulate and explain her intentions.

"What are you working on as a writer?" you'll ask. When you are working with second-graders, for sure, you'll teach children that when they respond to this question, you want to learn not just the writer's content ("my dog") or genre and content ("a poem about my dog") but also the writer's goals and strategies. ("I'm writing a poem about my dog *and I'm trying to make sure readers can visualize my dog, so I'm adding more descriptive words.*") Younger children can be prompted to answer more specific questions so that you learn not just the child's topic, but also the child's plans.

Often when conferring with a five- or six-year-old, then, you'll begin a conference by asking, "What are you working on as a writer?" However, because young children won't always be able to name their intentions, you will need to be especially careful to observe and examine their writing with an eye toward piecing together the child's intentions. Often, you'll say back what it is that you see the child doing, thereby giving the child words he or she can eventually use to articulate his or her intentions. You may, for example, say "I'm noticing that you are revising. It looks like you are adding details onto the main part—the most important thing—in your story. Is that right?"

If you ask, "What are you working on as a writer?" or any substitute for that question, and the child launches into the story of what she is writing about, you need to stop the child. It is okay to hold up your hand like the crossing guard at your school does to stop oncoming traffic. "Wait, wait," you'll need to say. Then you need to not just steer the child in a different direction but to explicitly say why you are doing this. "When I ask, 'What have you been working on as a writer?' I'm not really wanting to hear what you are writing about, though there will be times when I will ask you to tell me your content. I'm wanting to know what new stuff you are trying to do to get to be an even stronger writer. Like, for example, have you been . . . ," and then I might fill in some of the answers I anticipate the child producing.

Usually, once a child has told you what he or she is trying to do, you'll probe to understand what the child means. If the child says, "I'm revising to show, not tell," you are apt to say, "Can you show me where you did that?" or "What do you mean by this change here?" Of course, you usually have your own understanding of the terms children use (because they give you back the very terms you've taught them), but it is crucial to help a child articulate what *he or she* means by "I'm revising" or "I'm fixing up my ending." Sometimes you'll tell children what you notice, speculate about their intentions, and ask for their confirmation.

Of course, conferences occur in the context of previous conferences, so you can also begin a conference by recalling the last time you and the writer discussed his or her work, and you can ask, "How has it been, trying to do . . ." You can then look at progress that resulted from that conversation. For example, you might say, "Last time we talked, you agreed to take the giant step forward of shifting to new paper and trying to write a whole lot more. How has that been for you?" Then you'll follow up by saying, "Can we look at your work before we talked and since, and compare it?"

Make sure to pursue more than one line of questioning.

One of the rules of thumb that I especially emphasize is this: once you ask the writer a question about his or her writing and follow that line of questioning, you'll come to a place where you grasp one thing about the writer and his or her work. At this juncture, it is very tempting to launch into some teaching about that one point. Don't do it! Instead, suspend closure. Don't settle for a single line of inquiry. Be sure to return to a second question, following that one through so that you also understand another aspect of the writer and the work. If you first ask what the child is working on and learn about her work with the ending of a piece, for example, then say, "So one thing you are doing is working on an ending, and to do that you are . . . What are some of the *other* things you plan to do with this piece of writing today?" Of course, that second question could have been entirely different. You could have asked, "How do you feel about this piece? Is it one of your best? Is it just so-so?" You could have asked, "If you were going to fix this piece of writing up so that it is much, much better, what would you do?" As children think about their answers, you'll usually get a chance to sneak a quick look at the piece of writing so that as you interview the writer, you are also drawing on another source of information. One way or another, you will want several sources of information to draw upon as you move to the next phases of a conference.

In the research component of a conference, then, you observe, interview, and read the child's writing (though perhaps only a portion of it) to understand what the child is trying to do as a writer. Because your goal is to bring your students as far as possible along the writing path, and because you know that each conference is a precious opportunity to teach your students only one of the myriad of teaching points available, it is sometimes easy to get stuck doing research fixated on the many things the child does not yet know how to do. Of course, you do want to study what the child is not doing to help you decide what new thing to teach, but your conferences will be more successful and meaningful if you take in what the child is working on with your eyes open, particularly to his successes.

The Decision Phase

To an outside observer, a conference may seem fairly relaxed. But for me, as a teacher, conferences are anything but. As the young writer talks and as my eyes quickly take in the draft and any other available data, my mind is always in high gear. Malcolm Gladwell, the author of the best-selling book *Blink: The Power of Thinking without Thinking* (2007), suggests that he can observe a married couple for just half an hour and predict the chances that their marriage will be intact a decade hence. In a conference, I'm trying to do an equally astonishing feat of "thin-slicing." I take in all the data I can quickly assimilate, and as I do this, I'm theorizing, predicting, connecting this writer to other writers I've known, determining priorities, imagining alternate ways to respond, and lesson planning! All this must happen while I smile genially and act captivated enough by what the child says to keep the data coming my way! This is no easy task, and teachers are wise to recognize that this invisible aspect of teaching writing is the most challenging one of all.

In the decision phase of a conference, you'll quickly synthesize what you have learned and you'll think about the learning pathways that the child is traveling along. For example, a youngster is somewhere in a learning progression that relates to the type of text she is making. Relative to that, she is somewhere on the journey of learning to structure that kind of text, to elaborate on that kind of text. You need to ascertain where the writer is on that pathway so you can help her progress to the next step. You might say to the writer, "Hmm. You've told me a lot about your process and your writing plans. I need to think for a moment about what the most important coaching I can give you might be." It is important to deliberately delay acting on what you have learned until you have made a conscious decision. What is it you can teach that will make the biggest impact on this child's writing—not only in this instance but also in her whole life? There is no one right answer to this question, of course. In making this decision, you'll draw on the following considerations.

You want to teach every student to become someone who has intentions for his writing, assesses, sets a course, and acts deliberately.

Given that there is no one right way to improve any piece of writing, you'll want to listen to the writer's self-assessment, the writer's goals and plans, and to either teach within the context of the overall direction the writer has set or to talk to the writer about that overall direction. If the child thinks this is the best piece she has ever written and is working to copy it over exactly, you need to know the child's view before proceeding. When it makes sense to do so, you'll want to help the writer accomplish what he or she is already working to do—and perhaps to ramp up or extend those intentions.

If you don't want to get behind the child's existing intentions (or if you can't discern what these are), try to rally the child to take on a new intention *and then* equip the child to realize that intention.

If a child is writing in generalizations without any detail at all, you could simply elicit details and get the child to record them. But I suggest that, instead, you try *not* to do that, but rather first teach the child that writers try to write with details, rallying the child to embrace that goal. *Then* you can proceed to elicit those details and get them recorded on the page.

Responsive teaching doesn't mean that you simply buy into whatever a writer wants to do. Your teaching will be goal-driven. Your goals will come from your knowledge of the standards toward which you are teaching. It is your job to move youngsters to (and beyond) grade-level expectations. Your goals will come also from your own values and resolutions because your teaching can make a dramatic difference in supporting these. If it is important to you to support students' initiative, zeal, and willingness to take risks and to work hard, then these goals need to influence your ways of working in a conference.

Always teach toward growth—and eventual independence.

You will be thinking, "What is the most important way I can help this child to become a dramatically better writer?" You won't want your conference to be a time to spoon out a little thing that the child can accomplish within five minutes. Instead you will aim to help the child make a big step forward. On the other hand, the goal is for the child to be able to approximate this important work with independence, so you will balance wanting to challenge the writer with acknowledging that you need to teach what is next on this writer's horizon.

During the decision phase of a conference, you will also decide on *how* you will teach. You'll teach using one (and sometimes more than one) of the four methods described in Chapter 7: demonstration, guided practice, explanation with example, and inquiry.

The Teaching Phase

After you've made a decision about what and how you'll teach, you'll begin teaching. As you begin, you'll want to make sure to name an area of strength, something that the child has done (or has almost done) that has significance in the child's learning journey. You'll want to start teaching by naming this in a way that makes it likely that the child will do this same wise work again in future pieces of writing.

Name an area of writing strength; compliment the writer on a transferable skill or strategy.

To do this, you need to be able to extrapolate something transferable out of the details of the child's work. "I am noticing," you might say, "that you are rereading what you wrote before adding more words. That is so smart of you. Writers do that all the time!" Or "I love how you put so much detail into that picture of you and your cousin at the top of the Ferris wheel. I can even see your hair blowing in the wind! Writers do that, you know, add as much detail as they can into their writing so their readers can know even more about their stories." The challenge is to notice a very specific way the child has succeeded and then to phrase the compliment in such a way that the child knows something he or she can carry into his or her writing work on other pieces and other days.

If the child added into her draft the sound her guinea pig makes when it squeaks, you won't say, "I love that you added the 'ee, ee, ee' sound to your story. I hope you add that squeaking sound into your stories often!" Instead, you'll name what the child has done in a way that makes the action replicable: "I love the way you reread and added teeny details that could help readers create movies in their minds of exactly what happened. You made it so I can hear your guinea pig. Whenever you write, add details like these." Or "I love the way you've brought out dialogue—even if it is guinea pig dialogue! You didn't just say, 'Freddy made noises to greet me;' you told us exactly what he said!"

The best is if you can actually take in the new work that a youngster has tackled, the surprising power in his or her writing, and compliment something that represents the outer edge of the child's development. John Hattie's research suggests that compliments—what he refers to as *medals*—need to be informative. The point is not to pile on platitudes. It is to let a writer know that something he or she has been doing is really working—something the writer may not even realize he or she has been doing.

Teach and coach, reducing the scaffolding as you work together.

The teaching phase of a conference is remarkably similar to a minilesson. You'll make it clear that the conference has turned a corner and that you now want to explicitly teach the writer something that you hope will help her not only today, with this piece, but also in future writing projects. You might say something like, "Now, I'd like to give you one tip, one very important tip, that I think will help you not only with this piece but also with future pieces." Alternatively, you might say, "May I teach you one thing that I think will really, really help you a lot?" This helps the student know how to listen to what you are about to teach.

You'll word the teaching point in such a way that it can be generalized to other instances. For example, you might say, "One thing I do when I want to do what you are doing [convince my reader, write a really effective list, angle a story so that it makes a point] is . . ." Of course, you could refer to other writers rather than yourself: "Many writers find that to . . . it helps to . . . Specifically, they often. . . ."

Sometimes, after offering a strategy, you can ask the writer to either go off on his or her own and try the strategy you've just described or get started trying to do that work right now, as you watch (and coach). Often, though, you'll need to give an example from your own work or even show the writer what this might look like in her own work. The point will be to use whatever you have on hand to demonstrate the step-by-step process that a writer goes through to use the strategy to reach his goal.

Sometimes, after you give a quick demonstration yourself or show a quick example, you'll want the student to try the work while you watch and coach. For example, imagine the writer of an information book has written only one sentence of information about each of her subtopics, and you've suggested that she could reread the piece and star places where she could say more. In this case, you might suggest she point to a place in the text where she plans to write more and say aloud what she plans to write. Or, if you decide the writer needs more support, you might say, "So let's try this together," and then you could read aloud the relevant portion of the writer's draft, leaving spaces for the writer to do the new work. After helping—scaffolding—in that way, you'd note the child's progress and go through the work again, this time providing fewer scaffolds.

> "The single most important guideline to keep in mind in a conference is that the writer should leave wanting to write."

The Link Phase

Soon you will need to leave the child to work with independence. That is, after the writer has done a bit of work on her or his own (even if that work occurs in the conference, with the benefit of your scaffolding), you will want to step back and name what the writer has done that he can do again in another instance within this draft or when working on another piece of writing. "Keep going," you'll say at the end of the conference. You'll be sure to clarify the work the writer still needs to do. "Now that you have added all this information to the stuff you already wrote, do you think that when you write new things, you could write more about each thing? Maybe you could have one page be about one subtopic, the next page about the next subtopic . . ." As part of this, it is not uncommon for you to repeat the teaching point, this time not as a charge to the writer but as a record of what the writer has just done. As you remind the writer that it will be important to continue doing this good work often in future writing pieces, you'll explicitly support transference of what you have taught today into the child's ongoing independent writing process.

The challenge is to do all this, making sure the youngster's energy for writing goes up, not down. The single most important guideline to keep in mind in a conference is this: the writer should leave wanting to write.

When you follow the general pattern outlined here, conferences become more manageable. There will be some writing workshops where you spend your whole time conferring, in which case you can hold half a dozen intense, meaningful teaching interactions such as these, each one tailored to the individual needs of a child. More often, you'll divide your time between conferring and small-group work, holding half as many conferences and an equal number of small-group coaching sessions. As mentioned earlier, small-group coaching sessions follow a similar structure as one-to-one conferences, with some key differences. One difference is that the research and decision phases typically happen prior to pulling the small group of writers together. That is, you will have noticed several children struggling with a similar problem, for example, what to add and what to cut during revision, and you'll have already decided they would benefit from a small-group session. In this way, the research and decision phases happen on the run and prior to your small-group coaching. After establishing who—and what—you will teach, the teaching and link phases then follow a similar pattern as for one-to-one conferences, though typically there is a shorter demonstration or teaching point, followed by more time for students to practice the new skill or strategy as the teacher provides lean scaffolds, quickly moving from student to student. Other types of small-group sessions are centered around shared writing or inquiry. The benefits of pulling a small group together for a strategy session are that you can maximize your instruction across three or four students, observe closely as students practice the new strategy (providing lean directives as needed), and scaffolding children toward independence.

Whether you are spending most of the workshop conferring or splitting your time between conferring and small-group coaching sessions, the challenge is to lead effective conferences—quickly! Once you learn this general template, it will allow you to channel your attention and your thoughts to individual writers and to decide upon and support the specific next steps each child can take.

It is tremendously important that you confer regularly with children and that you do so in ways that teach children to confer with each other. You need to ask writers the questions that writers can profitably ask themselves. And you need, as much as possible, to hand over the conferences to the children, letting them become, with your support, both writer and reader, creator and critic.

Chapter 9

Supporting English Language Learners

BECAUSE THE TEACHERS COLLEGE Reading and Writing Project is deeply involved with schools where classrooms brim with English language learners, we spend a lot of time thinking about ways the writing workshop can be adjusted so that it is especially supportive for our ELLs. In many of our schools, teachers, coaches, and administrators have been working for decades on teaching writing and teaching language simultaneously throughout the workshop.

Balancing both—teaching writing and teaching language—is challenging, but greatly rewarding, for students and teachers. Many of the English learners in our classrooms are eager for the challenge. As their teachers, we need to find ways to communicate and help them access the information they need to grow in their language skills and give them lots of opportunities to write and speak in both their first language (if they are able) and in English. Some support for English learners is embedded in the framework of the writing workshop itself.

WAYS THE WRITING WORKSHOP ALREADY SUPPORTS ELLS

Consistent Teaching Structures

Workshop classrooms are organized in such clear, predictable, consistent ways that children quickly become comfortable participating in their ongoing structures. Very early in the school year, ELL children come to understand that writing workshops start with the teacher giving a minilesson, and that during the minilesson they learn strategies that they are then expected to apply to their independent work. Children know that after the minilesson they will be expected to write independently and that the teacher will circulate around the room, conferring with individuals and with small groups. Children also know that they will be expected at some point to share their work with a partner.

When the writing time is over, children know that they need to put their materials away and gather in the meeting area (or with a partner) for a share session. When teachers follow these routines day after day, students can focus their energies on trying to figure out how to do their work rather than on worrying over what they will be expected to do. The predictability of the workshop provides tremendous reassurance to a child who is just learning English, and this is amplified if workshop structures repeat themselves across other subjects.

Consistent Teaching Language

In addition, writing workshops are characterized by a consistent instructional language. The consistency of this language scaffolds each child's classroom experience, making it easier for a child who is just learning English to grasp the unique content that is being taught that day. For example, it helps that most minilessons start in a predictable manner, with teachers saying, "Writers," and then reviewing the content of previous minilessons, perhaps referencing a bullet on a chart. It helps children that every day the teacher encapsulates the day's minilesson in a sentence or two (the teaching point) that is repeated often and usually written on a chart.

Plentiful Opportunities for Writing Practice

Of course, the predictability of the workshop also means that teachers needn't invent a new way each day to support English language learners. Because the same classroom structures are in place every day, solutions that help on Tuesday will also help on Wednesday, Thursday, and Friday. This level of consistency, as well as predictability of activity and language, gives language learners not only a space for learning language, but also a place to practice. Whether your English language learner is a beginning speaker or advanced, she will have the opportunity to work on her writing and language skills each day. Repetition and practice are two important scaffolds that English language learners need to grow their literacy skills. They need to grow both their receptive language skills—their listening and reading—as well as their expressive language skills—their speaking and writing. The writing workshop is one more place where both of these skills can grow.

Differentiation through Choice and Social Interaction

Then, too, the work that children do in the writing workshop always, inevitably, provides wonderful learning opportunities for English language learners. Because the child usually chooses what she will write about, chooses the words she will use, chooses the people and places and topics and opinions that will be brought forth in the texts, chooses meanings that are vibrantly important to her, chooses the level of vocabulary and of sentence and text structures, and so forth, the writing workshop is *by definition* always individualized.

Here is the really powerful thing: the writing workshop is also, by definition, utterly interpersonal. You try it. Write about the things that are on your mind. Put your mom on the page or your son; capture that memory that haunts you or the topic you're an expert on; convince others that the cause or issue you are passionate about is worth their attention. Now bring this page to the table when you gather with the people who live and work alongside you. Share the text. Talk about it. You will find that by sharing your writing, something happens that makes you and the people with whom you live and work see each other in a new way; sometimes it will almost seem as if you are seeing each other for the first time. You will see that if you share your writing with your colleagues, you will go through each school day with a different sense of yourself and of your workplace, and the same will be true for your ELLs. You'll understand that song, "No man is an island, no man stands alone. Each man's joy is joy to me, each man's grief is my own." For every one of us, the chance to work and learn in the presence of a community of others is invaluable. Could we possibly give anything more precious to our English language learners? To all of our children?

Contextualized Exposure to New Genres, Structures, and Vocabularies

As students begin to write and think about their own stories, information texts, and persuasive essays, they will be given the opportunity over and over again to learn new vocabulary, use new language structures, and work on expressing their thoughts in a highly contextualized and pertinent situation. That is to say, they will be learning about language in a culturally relevant and high-interest activity, and writing about material that comes from their own lives and experiences.

USING ASSESSMENT TO TAILOR THE WORKSHOP AND PROVIDE EXTRA SUPPORT FOR ELLS IN ALL STAGES OF LEARNING ENGLISH

Of course, there is no such thing as "the" English language learner. Language learners, like all learners, differ one from the next in a host of ways. And remember, most of the kids in your classroom are language learners—especially in kindergarten and first grade—even if English is their first language. Two significant factors contributing to ELLs' unique needs, though, are the child's level of competence in his or her first language and the child's English proficiency.

Knowing where each student is in his or her English acquisition allows you to plan minilessons, confer with students, and set up supportive partnerships more strategically. Assessing your students' language proficiency, just as you assess their writing skills, is important to do so that you can identify goals and expectations that you will help them work toward in writing workshop. Ninety percent of the language that we have is acquired over time. So knowing what areas of language your ELLs know—for example, conversational English versus academic English—will help you coach your students during writing time. For language they don't know yet, you can create partnerships where they will hear those parts of language in context, and you can use those parts of language with kids during conferring and small-group sessions. Identifying language that kids use but confuse can help you identify goals that you can work on with kids, encouraging them to use those words with more effectiveness in their writing.

Most school districts have a language assessment, but every day in the writing workshop you are able to collect language samples, both written and oral. The more you look at the student and the language she uses throughout the day, in different contexts, the more you will be able to identify and support her to where she needs to move next linguistically.

It's critical that you think through how each of the components of a writing workshop can be altered to provide ELLs with the support they need. Most language learners go through predictable stages of language acquisition as they move to full fluency in English. When you plan the writing workshop, you need to think about how you are going to meet your children's needs as they develop English language skills and how you are going to adjust your expectations as children move toward full fluency. But let us think now about specific ways each of the components of the writing workshop can be altered just a bit so that the workshop as a whole is especially supportive for ELLs.

Support in the Preproduction and Early Production Stages of Learning English

When students are in the first few stages of language acquisition, they are generally working on learning such things as common nouns, prepositions, pronouns, and present tense.

Make your teaching and the words you use (students' words as well) as clear as possible.

You will want to help students build language in these areas by exposing them to language they can understand. What are some ways that you can make your teaching and talk more comprehensible to students?

- Use a lot of *visual examples in your teaching*. You might, for example, have in your demonstration piece a picture that shows the small moment you are writing about or an image that captures some of the information you are including in your piece. Sometimes I see teachers using their whole body when teaching a lesson, becoming highly animated. This is not only because animated teaching can grab and take hold of their students' attention, but also because doing so makes their teaching and language more comprehensible. These teachers use gestures, facial expressions, and intonation. In other words, they dramatize their teaching and talk to help make it more comprehensible.

- Offer students the use of *visual examples in their own writing*. In the beginning stages of language acquisition, whether working in English or their first language, students need to use pictures alongside their writing or pictures exclusively with some attempts to label. This way the teacher or the child's partner has something recognizable to talk about with him or her. Also, this allows students to write about things they do not necessarily have the vocabulary for yet. Pictures give the teacher as well as the community ways to know what the child is writing about and help aid communication between teacher and student.

Provide opportunities for listening and for learning the social language of the writing workshop.

Children who are in the silent period (preproduction stage) or in the early production stages of learning English have few oral English skills, but they will be listening carefully, trying to interpret what is going on around them. It is okay for children to be quiet at this stage, but it is important to understand that they are taking in a lot of information. The English words, phrases, and sentences that will make sense to them first will probably be the predictable sentences related to concrete classroom activities, such as "Get your writing," "Draw something on this paper," and "You can go to your seat now" or "Let's gather in the meeting area."

Opportunities for listening, really listening, are important, and the expectation that these children will participate in the comings and goings of the class spotlights the importance of them learning the social language that is most within their grasp. It is important that these children *are* being told, "Get out your pencil," "Draw here," and "Let's gather in the meeting area" (with accompanying gestures) and that they are expected to do all these things along with the others.

Establish partnerships and triads that support ELLs' burgeoning language development.

The writing workshop is an especially rich context for language development because children are not only writing and listening; they are also talking, and much of that talk happens in the small, supportive structures of partnerships. Eventually, these partnerships will give children important opportunities to rehearse for writing, but when children are in the preproduction stage of learning English, a partnership with one other child could make the child at the early production stage feel trapped, like a deer in the headlights, with nowhere to hide. Still, it is crucial that new arrivals are expected to join into the class as best they can from the start. There is never a time when new arrivals sit on the edge of the community, watching. Instead, the rug spot for the new arrival needs to be right in the center of the meeting area, and from the start, when children turn and talk during the active engagement section of a minilesson, these children must know that they belong to a conversational group.

Children in the early stages of learning English benefit from being in triads, not partnerships; ideally one child in that triad will share the new arrival's

native language but be more proficient in English, and the other child will be a native speaker of English (and a language model).

Granted, children who are in the preproduction stage of learning English will mostly listen. You can teach their more English-proficient partners how to use lots of gestures and to ask the child questions that can be answered with a yes or a no, a nod or a head shake.

You will want to coach your kids on how to work together in various configurations in the classroom. Many students benefit from meeting often with a peer to read their piece or talk about what it is that they have written and to get feedback on their writing. These conversations not only give them valuable feedback, but they also create opportunities for comprehensible language input from a peer. Many students in the first few stages of language acquisition also benefit from working with a partner to help them rehearse what they are going to write. Oral language rehearsal and practicing the words out loud is a wonderful strategy to help kids "work out" and test what they want to write. So often for our students, it takes a couple of times to think about how it might go on the page to help them find exactly what they want to say and how to say it. This is a good use of partner time in both the upper-grade and lower-grade classrooms.

Provide your ELLs opportunities to write in both their first language and in English.

When a child in the first stages of acquiring English arrives in a classroom, the first goal is to make sure that child is immediately active and interactive. If this child is literate in his or her first language, then by all means it is important for the child to write (and to read) in that language. If there are people in the classroom or the school who can speak the child's native language, you can rely on this buddy to convey to the child the kind of text that the class is writing, and some of the main qualities of that type of writing. For example, this buddy might convey, "We are writing about our opinions, about how we liked or didn't like the book we just read, and a few reasons why."

Whether or not the new arrival is literate in his first language, you will want that child to write as best he can in his first language, while also offering him opportunities to begin doing some writing in English. Some teachers find that it helps for these children to have time slots for first-language writing and for English writing, with the child perhaps starting the writing workshop with fifteen minutes to write in his first language. (During this time, the child can write with volume that is comparable to other children and build his identity as a child who writes a lot.) But it is also important for this child to write in English.

Usually we start by asking the child who is at an early stage of learning English to draw and label her drawing when writing in English. This, of course, is what we ask kindergarten and first-grade children to do as a matter of course. After a child has drawn and labeled in English for a bit, you can ask the child to start writing in sentences. These children need the same range of paper choices that you normally offer to children in earlier grades (for example, a second-grade ELL may need the same paper choices that are offered to kindergarten or first-grade children). It is especially important that these children have access to paper that contains a large box on the top of a page and several lines for writing under that box. The size of the box shrinks and the number of lines increases as children develop proficiency in English. This progression of paper choice is an extremely powerful way to scaffold children's language development. Imagine that the child has written about a soccer game in her first language and drawn a series of sketches showing what happened first, next, and last in the game. Then, with help from English-speaking peers, the child labels each drawing with lots of English words, providing herself with a picture dictionary that is tailored to that her exact story. It is not such a big step, then, to ask this child to use those words and write a sentence or two to accompany each of her drawings.

Plan instruction with your ESL instructor to maximize learning in the writing workshop.

If you have children who are in the early stages of English acquisition, it is especially important to provide them with extra help understanding the content of a minilesson. If there is an English as a second language teacher who is willing to provide support, this can also be extremely beneficial. Some ESL teachers push in to classrooms; some ESL teachers pull out children for work in the ESL room. While not always possible, we recommend that ELLs remain in the classroom to maximize interaction and instructional opportunities. In either case, working in tandem with your ESL teacher will benefit your ELLs.

If classroom teachers and ESL teachers are provided with opportunities for planning together, the ESL teacher can support the children during writing workshop by preteaching the concepts and developing the vocabulary that will be necessary to understand what will be taught in the minilesson. For example, if the minilesson will teach children how to write with main ideas and support ideas, the ESL teacher might use a nonfiction content-area book and lots of gestures to convey that the title of the book is the main idea or the big idea, and then to convey that some of the subtitles are support ideas (or smaller ideas). The teacher could reinforce the concept of ordination and subordination (without using those terms) by showing that if the classroom represents a big topic, the library area could represent a subtopic.

Many ESL teachers also work with groups of students to help target specific parts of language. They may use shared writing or interactive writing as way to build language structures that relate to the unit of study that students are in. Many teachers also then conduct group conferences with students who are working on the same parts of language.

Create concise minilessons that rely on visuals and familiar references.

There are other ways to alter minilessons to support English language learners. First, you will want your minilessons to be as concise as possible. If you are working with a large ELL population, you'll want to trim the minilessons in this series! Then, too, visuals can make a huge difference. It helps to draw and act as you talk. Sketch almost any story, information book, or persuasive text as you tell it. If you want to describe the way a writer can "stretch out" sections of a story, for example, it helps to tug on the ends of a rubber band whenever saying the term *stretch out*. You will also probably make a special point of using examples that children can relate to. It's also helpful to repeat the teaching point more often with children who are learning English. Similarly, when you want children to turn and talk, it can help to set them up with cue cards. In a persuasive unit, for example, you might give them cards that say "one reason . . ." and "another reason. . . ."

Support in the Later Stages of Learning English

It is important to celebrate the work that children at this stage of early emergent English are producing, focusing on the content and quality of their spoken and written texts, not only on the correctness of the syntax. These children are taking risks, and your job is to help them to feel successful.

Move students in this stage from triads to partnerships or pair them with an early emergent ELL.

As children begin to acquire more fluency in English, they will be able to understand written and spoken English when they have concrete contexts (pictures, actions, sounds, and so on). As they develop these proficiencies, you might move them from triads to partnerships (or nudge them to become one of the more vocal members of a triad, with a new preproduction ELL joining in as best as he or she can). You know these learners will not always use correct syntax but also know they can participate fully in partnership work. Remember that all language learners need the best language models possible. So as your determine your partnerships and triads you will want to keep this in mind.

Extend on the language ELLs are producing.

As children become more proficient in English, their answers to questions will become more extended, but of course their hold on English grammar and vocabulary will still be approximate. Again, partners (and teachers) can be coached to realize that this is not a time for correcting grammar. Instead, it is a time for extending what the child says. If the child points to a picture she has drawn as part of a story she's written and says, "Mom," then you'll want to expand on this. "That's your mom?" Pause for a nod. "You and your mom," pointing, "went in the car?" Point again. "Where did you go?" Gesture to illustrate that the question pertained to where the car drove. If the child isn't sure how to answer, you can eventually supply options, "Did you go to the store? Or to the park?"

Scaffold children's writing with conversational prompts.

To help children bring a growing repertoire of language from the minilessons into their independent work, you might scaffold the writing that children do (and also the conversations that children have during work time with their partners) by providing them with conversational prompts. For example, in an opinion unit, you might teach children to write or say, "I see . . ." and then to shift and write or say, "I think . . ." The thought can be elaborated on when the child learns to use transition phrases such as *for example*. Children who are just learning English may rely heavily on these prompts, and you may even write cue cards for them.

Provide time for in-context grammar instruction.

While it is important to support children's attempts at emerging syntax, children also need instruction. For example, if children are writing personal narratives, you might teach and then post transition words that show that a little time has passed, such as *then, later, after a while, five minutes later*, or *next*. You might remind children that in their stories or essays, as they move from one moment in time to the next, they will often use a transition word to show that time has passed. To practice this, you might ask one partner to tell another what he or she did since walking in the classroom, remembering to insert words that show the passage of time. When partners meet, you can suggest that they talk through the sequence of events in each child's writing, using transition words as the storyteller or essayist progresses from one moment in time to the next. Each child will also benefit from having a list of these transition words during work time.

Support in Learning Academic English

As important as it is for you to tailor work time during the writing workshop so that children in the early stages of English acquisition receive the help they need, it is equally important for you to be cognizant that children who are in later stages of language acquisition also need special support. When children reach intermediate fluency, they demonstrate increased levels of accuracy and are able to express their thoughts and feelings in English. They often sound as if their English is stronger than it is. This is because although these children have developed conversational skills, often they still do not have academic English language skills. These children often seem to be very proficient in English. They have a strong command of social English and can use English to chat with each other, to learn what the teacher expects them to do, and to talk about the events of the day. They may sound fluent in social conversation where complex structures can be avoided, but it is often difficult to follow them when they describe events from another time and place.

One way to determine whether a child needs help with academic English is to talk to the child about the story in a novel or about something that happened in another time and place. Invite the child to retell an episode from the book or from the child's experience; listen well. If the child's language is such that you have a hard time really piecing together what she is intending to communicate, chances are good that this child needs support with academic English. The term *academic English* does not refer only to the language that is used in discipline-based studies. It refers to the language that a person must use to communicate about times and places that are distant and unfamiliar and that must be created by words.

The challenge for these children is that they need now to learn academic English; to do this, they need input from people who can provide strong language models and from skilled teachers.

Scaffold students' work on elaboration and writing with description and specificity.

At this stage it is very important for teachers to work on elaboration and specificity to help children use more descriptive and extended language. It is also important for these children to be partnered with children for whom English is their first language, children who can function as strong language models. Often, when teachers have a handful of children who are in the earliest stages of language acquisition and a handful who are further along, teachers devote most of their special attention to the children who are the newest to English. However, if you set new arrivals up with the proper invitations to work, support structures from other children, and ways of being interactive, they can learn a huge amount from each other. Meanwhile, you can devote your time to children who have a good command of social English but not of academic English and need help that is less readily available from the peer group.

Provide explicit instruction in tenses, pronoun references, connectors, and so on.

Children who need help with academic English will profit from explicit instruction tailored to their needs. For example, these children benefit from instruction in connectives. They tend to write in simple sentences, linked together with the connector *and*. It is important for children to study connectors, because when English language learners learn to read as well as to write, these can become a source of confusion. Many readers assume that sentences are arranged in chronological order. However, in many sentences, that assumption is incorrect; for example, "I went to the office because the principal called for me over the PA system." In small-group instruction, then, you will want to provide English language learners with explicit instruction to help them understand connectors, tenses, pronoun references, and so forth.

Support students in building vocabulary using their own writing as the context.

Of course, English language learners also need support in developing a rich vocabulary, and, again, these children benefit from explicit instruction. If a child overuses a word such as *nice* or *beautiful*, you will want to help him learn that there are many different, more precise words the child could use. Is the person lovely? Impressive? Unusual? Dignified? Cute? Some teachers help children to develop word files, with the overused word at the center of a card and five variations of that word around the edges. Children keep these cards on hand throughout the day and look for opportunities to use specific words orally (some teachers ask children to place a check mark beside a word each time they use it orally).

This word bank should also be on hand when the child writes. If a child decides that her beloved mother is not cute but dignified, then the child's personal connection to the word will make it more memorable than had the child merely encountered it in a class on vocabulary.

Similarly, if children are writing about a particular subject, the teacher or an English-speaking buddy may want to help the child build a domain-specific vocabulary to draw upon as he or she writes. If the child is writing about attending a carnival, the child would benefit from having a conversation about her experience at the carnival. This sort of rehearsal is important to every writer, but it can provide extra language support to the English language learner who is ready to learn precise vocabulary.

Provide small-group instruction for students to learn figurative language.

Children learning academic English will also need support as they come to understand and use figurative language. Of course, literature is filled with metaphors and similes, as are the minilessons in this series. Children who are just on the brink of learning academic English will profit from some small-group instruction that gives them access to literary devices.

YOUR TEACHING IN EVERY UNIT CAN SUPPORT WRITING GOALS—AND LANGUAGE GOALS

When you approach a unit of study, you need to think about the language needs of ELL children in the classroom: what are the language skills that your children need to have to understand the work they are being asked to do? You need to think not only about the writing skills and strategies that will be developed in a unit but also about the language skills the unit will support. You need to think about the vocabulary, the idiomatic expressions, the connectives, the conjunctions, and about the grammar you want children to develop in a unit. There has to be a plan for content and a plan for language, side by side.

When approaching a unit on information writing, for example, you can anticipate that you'll be teaching children to explain, describe, compare, categorize, and question. You can anticipate that mostly you'll be helping children write in present tense and that they'll benefit from learning connectives such as *if*, *when*, *because*, *for example*, *another example*, and so forth. You can plan that you might provide scaffolds such as a chart of phrases, and you can know in advance that children may need help with instructional terms such as *fact*, *example*, *type*, *reason*, and *description*. You know you may teach the language of comparison, including, for example, the use of the *er* and *est* word endings, as in *big*, *bigger*, *biggest*.

The power of written curriculum is that you and a group of colleagues can hold your hopes for teaching in your hands and talk and think together about how you can take your own best ideas and make them better. One of the most important ways to make your teaching stronger is to think, "How can we give all children access to this teaching?" The wonderful thing about a workshop is that it is incredibly supportive for English language learners, but if you bring your best ideas to the table, you can make the writing workshop even more supportive.

Chapter 10

Building Your Own Units of Study

THIS SERIES WILL HAVE DONE ITS JOB WELL if it not only helps you to *teach the units* described to good effect, but if it also encourages you to work collaboratively with your colleagues to *author your own units of study*. In their new book, *Professional Capital* (2012), Michael Fullan and Andy Hargreaves point out that master teachers not only study and learn *best* practices; they also have the skills, the knowledge, and the confidence to develop the *next* practices. This series has been carefully constructed with an eye toward teaching you to author your own units of study in writing.

In this chapter, I will pass along what I've learned about the process of developing curriculum in hopes that this can help you and your colleagues create units of study that fill gaps that we have left in the curriculum. You'll want to be in a position to respond to priorities in your region, and to your students' interests and your own, by authoring units that aren't described in Units of Study for Teaching Writing. The book *If . . . Then . . . Curriculum: Assessment-Based Instruction* will help you imagine some possible units, suggesting broad contours of those suggested units, and I hope some of those units appeal to you so that our unit summaries are able to function as a scaffold, supporting you as you develop your own writing curriculum. But I also know that you will want to develop your own units of study from scratch; this chapter can help you do that.

DECIDE ON THE SUBJECT FOR YOUR UNIT OF STUDY

First, of course, you will need to decide on what it is you will teach. You will see that the units that we've detailed in this series tend to be genre-based; genre is one of the great organizers of writing. Genre is a rather obvious way to organize students' work with writing. It is easier to imagine planning a unit of study on a kind of writing—whether that writing consists of persuasive reviews or how-to books—than on a part of the writing process or a quality of good writing because units on a particular genre will inevitably encompass the full span of the writing process. In a genre study, students begin to imagine what they will be writing by doing some reading; then they rehearse, draft, revise, and edit that kind of writing—either progressing through one cycle or through many cycles of writing, producing one finished text or many. Certainly there are many genres that have not been addressed in the current series. Some of these—such as informational books in science, pattern books, and songs—have been sketched out in *If . . . Then . . . Curriculum*, but many others remain as wide open terrain.

But it is also important for you to understand that you can design units of study that are not genre-based. For example, you could design a unit of study on revision, channeling students to review their folders full of writing and to select several pieces from throughout the year that deserve to be revised, then helping them set to work with those pieces of writing. In a similar way, you could conceivably design a unit of study on a topic such as author studies. This, like a unit on revision, could involve students revising pieces they wrote earlier in the year, this time doing so under the influence of authors. Alternatively, you could develop a unit focusing on a quality of good writing. For example, you could rally children to closely study places where authors "show, not tell." Children could then revise their existing texts to show, not tell, more often, and eventually they could draft new texts, using all they've learned. There are other qualities of good writing I could imagine studying: characterization, for example, or the development of reasons and examples to support an opinion.

Then, too, you could study a social structure that supports writing. For example, you could design a unit of study called "Writing Friendships," in which you help children consider how to work well with a partner and perhaps with a writing club. How might a writing partnership best help with rehearsal for writing? With drafting? With revision?

Although it is possible to design units of study on topics such as these rather than on genre, these topics will be more challenging. If you have experience developing units of study for writing, have a mentor working closely with you, or if you are following one of the plans laid out in your grade's *If . . . Then . . . Curriculum* book, you might decide to try your hand at such a unit. In the absence of these supports, I suggest you may want to start by developing a genre-based unit of study.

In any case, take some time to mull over possible topics for the unit, guarding against the temptation to seize on the first topic of study that comes to mind.

Clarify your goals by thinking about what unit of study would especially benefit your children, keeping in mind what they can do and almost do.

When you decide upon a unit of study, you are taking it upon yourself to channel the young people in your care to devote at least a month of their writing lives toward the topic that you settle upon. Therefore, it is important to weigh whether a particular topic will be especially beneficial for children. When a unit of study comes to mind, you'll want to put it through the test of asking a few hard questions. Start by asking, "Will the skills students develop during this unit of study be important ones for them? Will the unit be a high-leverage one, setting youngsters up to do similar work in other genres or in other areas of the curriculum?" For example, perhaps a teacher decides that she wants her children to become more skilled at writing proficient first-draft writing on demand. For this reason, she may decide to turn the classroom into a newsroom and teach children to write news articles and editorials. That decision makes sense.

It goes without saying that you need to believe that any unit of study that you teach (any unit you impose upon your children) must be incredibly important. You probably won't want to channel all of your students to spend a month or six weeks of time working on a genre that doesn't seem to you as if it will provide students with skills that will be foundational or transferable. For example, a unit on limericks or sea shanties or haiku might be fun, but before embarking on such a unit, I'd want to weigh whether it would pay off as much as other units.

Then, too, think about how the unit relates to your students' skill levels in relation to standards for their grade and to their zone of proximal development. As you think about this, you'll find yourself honing in on what, exactly, you will be teaching within the topic. For example, one could teach a unit on nonfiction chapter books that reminded students of what they already know about the structure of information writing and that focused especially on research—on collecting and integrating information from a wide variety of sources and synthesizing that information into coherent texts. Alternatively, a unit on nonfiction chapter books could help students write what they already know—about topics they are already experts on—with an emphasis on the essentials of information writing. In the same way, if you were to teach a unit on revision, the decision to address that topic wouldn't, alone, provide a clear direction for your unit. Do you want to focus on students writing to discover new insights or on the physical tools for (and reasons for) adding to and subtracting from a text and the challenges of elaboration? Of course, you could select an entirely different focus altogether for a unit on revision. My point, only, is that once you decide upon the terrain for the unit of study you will teach, you still need to hone in on specific skills, and to do that, you need to know your students well and to think hard about their entire writing curriculum.

For example, if you and your colleagues decided to develop a unit of study on poetry, you'd want to think about how that unit would fit into earlier and later work across students' school careers on poetry—and on writing in general. You would want to take some time to create a gradient of difficulty for studying poetry. What might be more accessible for younger writers? More demanding for older writers? You might, for example, decide that for more novice writers, a unit on poetry could highlight reading-writing connections and revision, and for more proficient writers, a unit on poetry could highlight imagery and metaphor. Of course, both reading-writing connections and metaphor can be taught in simpler or more complex ways, so you and your colleagues might decide instead to study imagery and metaphor across the grades, with increasing levels of sophistication and challenge.

Here is a final word about one's choice of a unit of study: the other deciding factor is you. If you are learning to play the guitar and find yourself dying for the chance to dig into song writing, then consider bringing that passion into the classroom. If you loved teaching your fiction unit and yearn to do more, consider a unit on revision, or on character development (which could invite children to revise several earlier pieces to bring the characters to life more), or writing gripping fictional stories with meaning and significance. In the end, children can grow as writers within any unit of study. And whether you are teaching a unit on independence in the writing workshop or on writing to change the world, you need to remember in particular that you are teaching children and teaching writing. The rest is negotiable.

PLAN THE WORK CHILDREN WILL DO

It is tempting to start planning a unit of study by writing a minilesson for Day One and then for Day Two. What I have found is that if I proceed in that manner, chances are great that those intricate, time-consuming plans will end up being jettisoned.

I recommend instead that you begin by thinking about the work that you envision your children doing in this unit. For example, before you can imagine the unit's flow, you need to decide whether children will be writing one piece during the unit or two or many. Assuming children are cycling through the writing process more than once, writing more than one text, will they work the whole time on one kind of writing, or will they start with one kind of writing before switching to another kind? For example, in one unit students begin by writing information chapter books and end by writing feature articles; in another they begin by writing persuasive speeches and end by writing petitions and letters. Also, you need to decide whether writers will proceed in synchronization with one another or whether some children will write three texts and some only one. Then, too, you need to decide whether you imagine children progressing quickly through rehearsal, spending more time on revision, or vice versa.

"Remember that you are teaching children and teaching writing. The rest is negotiable."

We always spend a lot of time constructing a storyline through the unit, one that orients the bends in the road of the unit. The storyline needs to account for whether this is a new genre for students and, if so, whether you will take students through a scaffolded, shared writing experience before launching them into generating their own topics or story ideas, with a clear expectation of producing rough essays, narratives, nonfiction chapter books, or free writing. That is, the arc of the unit—what children will be writing, how long they will spend on that writing, and when you will give them more independence and when more scaffolding will be necessary—needs to be outlined before you can start writing minilessons.

When planning the work that students will do, it is important to think about the progression of endeavors that they might possibly take on, choosing work that will be challenging for the class, but not so challenging that they are brought to a halt. For example, when considering how to help students write lab reports and science books on forces of motion, we knew that the unit was a challenging one. Students would be writing about content they probably didn't have a real strong handle on, and they'd be wrestling with sources and domain-specific vocabulary in ways that would be challenging. And what, really, could we reasonably expect them to write early on in the unit?

We decided to first channel children to write hypotheses and procedures to their experiments. In this way, students would not be expected to elaborate on focused topics in ways that would be especially difficult. Next, we imagined that students might go back to their lab reports, making them more precise by using domain-specific vocabulary before moving on to write science chapter books. We wanted to give students a goal that we knew would be doable for them. We knew, too, that by the time students met that goal, they'd be ready for a new and more challenging one. This next goal, of course, required more choice as well as more complexity. Students would be ready to handle those challenges because they stood on the shoulders of the earlier work.

It helps to imagine different ways that the unit of study you've selected might proceed, and then weigh the pros and cons of those various alternatives. Whatever the genre, whatever the form, there are some principles that underlie the progressions in most units. Early in the unit, students generally work with synchronicity to complete one or sometimes two pieces of writing. During this phase, we do a lot of instruction, and that teaching is captured on anchor charts. Then in most units, we ask students to transfer what they have learned to the work they do writing a new text. They work on the new text with new levels of independence, and they not only apply all they learned during the first portion of the unit, but they also stand on the shoulders of that early work to reach for more demanding goals.

These are a few common templates, then, for a unit of study.

- Your children might generate lots of one kind of writing, perhaps taking each bit of writing through a somewhat limited amount of revision. Then your children look back over all of that writing to choose one piece (presumably from the writing they've only lightly revised) to delve into with more depth, bringing it to completion. After this, students work on the entire cycle of writing, this time working under the influence of a mentor text, aiming to do all they did previously, only better now, as they emulate published work.

- Your children may start with an intensive two-day immersion in the kind of writing they will be doing in the unit, doing this work with lots of support

from you. Then, all the members of the class work in synchronism on their own writing project. This project contains lots of parts or steps, and you coach writers along each step (or aspect) of the piece. After completing that one main project, students fast-draft a quicker version of that project.

Let's imagine that you decide to teach a unit on poetry. You'd probably find this fits best into the first template. Presumably, at the start of the unit, each child could write and lightly revise a bunch of poems. Then, writers could commit themselves to taking one poem (or a collection of poems that address one topic) through more extensive revision and editing. They could then work through a similar cycle, perhaps this time writing a poetic picture book, not a poem. A unit of study on news articles could fit into that same template. News stories are written quickly, so children could generate many of these at the start of the unit, bringing more and more knowledge to them as they learn more. Then, you could explain that sometimes a writer decides to extend the news article into a more developed sort of writing, and you could teach children to rewrite one of their articles into an investigative report or an editorial (either project would require more research and revision).

On the other hand, you might decide that within one unit, children will work on a single, large writing project, say a piece of literary nonfiction, perhaps one requiring research. Perhaps for this unit, each child will investigate a different endangered species. You may decide that the first half of the unit will focus not on drafting information writing but on note-taking. Then, during the second half of the unit, children could draft their literary nonfiction. The unit might end with you teaching writers that the work they do when writing feature articles is not unlike the work of writing literary nonfiction books and with all children working on a quick cycle to write feature articles.

My larger point is that before I write a single minilesson, I bring out a blank calendar for the unit and plan how the children's work is apt to unfold across the month or six weeks. If I imagine that for the first week or week and a half in a unit, children will gather entries—I mark those days onto the calendar. I do not yet know the specific minilessons I will teach, but I do know the broad picture of what children will be doing during those days. Proceeding in a similar fashion, I mark off the bends in the road of a unit. Even after this, however, I'm still not ready to write minilessons.

GATHER AND STUDY TEXTS FOR CHILDREN TO EMULATE

Before actually embarking on writing the minilessons in a unit of study, I generally gather and select examples of the sort of text I hope children will write. That is, if you decide to teach a unit on writing editorials and to emphasize the importance of the counterargument, you'll want to turn your classroom library upside down looking for examples of the sort of thing you plan to teach. You'll become a magnet for this sort of writing and find examples of it throughout your life. You will very likely want to invite your children to join you in this, depending on where they are in their writing and reading lives at the time.

Soon you will have gathered a pile of writing, and you can begin to sift and sort through it, thinking:

- What are the different categories of texts here?
- What are the defining features of this sort of writing?
- Which of these texts could become exemplars for the unit of study?

To make these decisions, you'll need to think not only about the texts but also about your kids and about the standards that your school has adopted. You will want to aim toward goals that are achievable for your students, and you will also want to be sure that over the course of the school year, your students meet the standards your school has adopted. For me, this means teaching in ways that are aligned to the Common Core State Standards.

Although I often gather a small stack of relevant texts, I generally select just two or perhaps three to use with children during any one unit of study. To decide upon the texts that you will use as exemplars for the unit, you'll need to take into consideration the particular focus you will bring to this unit. For example, when I taught children to write fiction, I knew that I wanted their stories to involve just two or three characters and to take place across just two or three small moments. I knew, also, that I wanted the fiction to be realistic fiction. Fiction comes in all shapes and sizes, so I needed to do some research before settling upon Henry and Mudge in first grade and *The Leaving Morning* and *Owl Moon* in second grade.

Often, you will decide to use your own writing as one of the touchstone texts for the class, and you might also decide to use writing done by another child another year. These are perfectly reasonable choices. When teaching students to write personal essays or literary essays or research-based argument essays, it is unlikely that you'll find published work that closely resembles the work you expect children to produce, so your own writing becomes especially important in instances such as these.

When teaching, it is important to have more than one text to weave through minilessons. In some units, for example, I often demonstrate by referencing a piece of my own writing, but meanwhile, during the active engagement section of many minilessons, I set children up to practice what I've demonstrated by channeling them to work on a class piece. Before you begin a unit of study, then, you may want to consider not only what the exemplar texts will be that thread throughout the unit, but also whether kids will work collaboratively on a class text.

READ, WRITE, AND STUDY WHAT YOU WILL TEACH

I describe units as if they are courses of study for children, and of course, the truth is they are courses also for us! In addition to collecting examples of the sort of writing you'll be asking kids to do, you will also want to scoop up all the professional books and articles you can find pertaining to your unit of study. You can learn a lot from books for adult writers, so don't limit yourself to books by and for teachers.

I cannot stress enough that you need to do the writing that you are asking your kids to do. You needn't devote a lot of time to this. The writing that you use as an exemplar text needs to be very brief anyhow, so even ten minutes of writing, four times a week, will give you tons of material to bring into your minilessons. The important thing is, that during those ten minutes, you work in very strategic ways. Usually, you'll begin with a bare-bones small text, and you'll develop or revise it in exactly the same ways that you suggest your kids try.

As you read and write, try to think about ways the current unit of study could build on previous learning. Not everything that you and your kids do in this unit can be brand-new. What is it that kids already know that they can call upon within this unit? What will the new work be?

Think, also, about what is essential in the unit and what is more detailed work. The answer to that question lies not only in the unit itself, but in your hopes for how this unit of study will help your kids develop as writers. If you are teaching poetry with a hope that this will lead children toward being able to engage in much more extensive revision, then this goal will influence your decision about what is essential in the unit.

OUTLINE A SEQUENCE OF TEACHING POINTS

After all this preparation, it will finally be time to outline a sequence of teaching points. When I do this, I am usually not totally sure which teaching points will become minilessons and which will become mid-workshop teaching points or share sessions. Those decisions often come very late, as I revise my unit.

You will want to make your plans within general time constraints. For example, I might say to myself, "I will use about three days for teaching kids to highlight the central ideas in their information writing." You'll approach a set of days, then, feeling sure about the most important skills that you want to teach and the most important content you want to convey. Then you'll decide on strategies that will help students be able to do this work. For example, in this instance, I decided that to help students highlight the central ideas in their information writing, I should teach them to reread their writing, looking for the ideas they want to especially highlight, to stretch out the parts of their writing related to those ideas, to use introductory sentences and topic sentences to highlight those ideas, and to use text features in ways that accentuate the shared ideas. In this way, I had that progression of teaching in mind before beginning to write specific minilessons.

Before you can write minilessons, you also need to name or invent some practical, how-to procedure that you believe young writers can use to achieve a goal. For example, if I want children to use text features to highlight what a text is really about, I need to decide how to go about teaching students to do that. Maybe I'll use a mentor text to show them how another author has done that, or I'll recruit the class to work together on using text features to highlight central ideas in our class text. Once you figure out one way that youngsters can do whatever it is you want to help them to do, you are ready to teach them this strategy in a minilesson or a mid-workshop teaching point or a share.

Of course, whenever you teach anything worth teaching, you need to anticipate that kids will encounter trouble. When I teach kids ways to highlight the central ideas in information writing, for example, I need to anticipate that this will pose difficulties for some kids. At least half your teaching does not involve laying out brand-new challenges but instead involves coaching and supporting kids through predictable challenges.

When you plan a unit of study, you'll find that it is crucially important to anticipate the difficulties kids will encounter in the unit. You'll want to plan to provide students with the scaffolding necessary to have success with first a pared-down version of what you are teaching and, eventually, with higher-level work. For example, I was pretty sure I would need to provide some scaffolding for kids when I taught them that they could reread an essay as if they were in a plane, looking down at the structure and the overall chunks of text. When I told kids to look at the patterns of chunks and think, "What was the author doing in this chunk of text?" and "What about in this one?" I knew that some children would find this confusing. To scaffold children's efforts to do this, I boxed out the major sections of a text I found, explaining my thinking about the work each chunk was doing. Then I asked children to try this with another text, which I'd already boxed into sections.

Although you can anticipate lots of the difficulties that kids will encounter as you teach them, it is inevitable that new issues will emerge. So you'll keep your ears attuned and your eyes alert. As you teach a unit, you'll outgrow yourself and your best teaching plans in leaps and bounds.

WRITE MINILESSONS

In writing workshops, kids generate ideas for writing, and then they select one of those to develop. They make an overall plan on either a timeline, a table of contents, or some boxes and bullets, and then they revise those plans. They try a few alternative leads—and then get started. They write with some tentativeness, expecting to revise what they write with input from others.

The process of authoring a unit of study is not so different. You'll generate an overall plan for the unit and revise it. Eventually you'll settle on a plan and get started. After all that planning and revising, you'll write the first word. Even then, you'll write knowing that your teaching plans will be what Gordon Wells refers to as "an improvable draft."

If teaching plans are only in your mind, or only coded into a few words in a tiny box of a lesson-plan book, then it's not easy to revise those plans. But ever since human beings were cave dwellers, inscribing the stories of hunts on stony cave walls, we have learned that once we record our thoughts and plans, the community can gather around those thoughts. Those thoughts can be questioned, altered, and expanded. The ideas of one person can be added to the thoughts of another. In scores of schools where I work closely with teachers, we keep a binder for each unit of study. In that binder, we keep a collection of all the minilessons written that are related to each unit. Many of these are minilessons one teacher or another wrote, but others come from professional development teachers have attended or books they've read. In these binders, the teachers also deposit other supporting material.

Hints for Writing Minilessons

The Start of the Connection

Try to think of the first part of your connection as a time to convey the reason for this minilesson. You are hoping to catch children's attention and to rally their investment. Sometimes, this is a time to step aside from writing for just a moment, telling a story or reliving a class event in a manner that will soon become a lead to (or metaphor for) whatever you will teach. Then, too, this is often a time to rally kids to recall and apply what they have already learned that functions as a foundation for this new instruction. If you have trouble writing the start of a minilesson, it is also possible to settle for simply saying, "Yesterday I taught you . . ." and then referring to the exact words of that teaching point. These should usually be written on a chart, so gesture toward the chart as you talk. Ideally, you can follow this with a memorable detail of someone who used the strategy or applied the teaching point during the preceding day's minilesson. This memorable point may be something a published author, you, or a child said or did. You can say something such as, "Remember that. . . ."

The Teaching Point

The teaching point will be only a few sentences long, but nevertheless it merits care and revision; it is the most important part of your minilesson. Plan to repeat the exact words of your teaching point at least twice in the minilesson. To learn to create teaching points, try temporarily staying within the template of these words or something very close to them: "Today I will teach you that when writers . . . , they often find it helps to . . . They do this by. . . ." The important thing to notice in this template is that we are not saying, "Today we will do this." A teaching point is not the assignment for the day! Instead,

the teaching point is a strategy that writers often use to accomplish important writing goals. Then, too, notice that teaching points do not simply define the territory within which one will teach. That is, if a teaching point went like this: "Today I will teach you how to write good leads," then there would be nothing worth remembering in this teaching point!

The Teaching

When planning how the teaching will go, begin by deciding what your method and materials will be. If you will be demonstrating using your own writing, go back and look at a few minilessons in which I used a similar method, and at first, follow the template of these minilessons. You will probably see that I set children up to participate or to observe. Then, I either tell the story of how I came to need the strategy and act out what one does first and next in using this strategy, or I recruit youngsters to join me in trying to use the strategy. Once youngsters are participating, I do my work in ways that allow them to watch what I do and compare my work to what they were en route to doing. I often include in my demonstration an instance when I did something unhelpful, and then I correct myself, getting back on track. Throughout the demonstration, I tend to write only about four sentences; usually these are added to an ongoing piece that threads its way through much of the unit.

I might demonstrate using a bit of a published author's text instead of my own writing; again, if you decide to create a minilesson using that method, find instances when I did this and let them serve as exemplars for you. You'll find that if I am demonstrating using a published author's text, I'll enact what the author probably did, prefacing my enactment with a phrase like, "So-and-so probably did this. He probably. . . ."

I might choose not to demonstrate. Instead, for example, I might explain something and then show an example. These kinds of minilessons are more challenging to write, but again, I encourage you to find and follow a model as a way to induct yourself into this work.

The Active Engagement

Almost always, the active engagement is a time when children try the strategy that you have just taught, and they do so by writing-in-the-air to a partner. For example, if you have taught that toward the end of their work on a text, writers reread their own writing to ask, "Does this make sense?" then you'll want to use the active engagement time as a chance to provide children with some scaffolded practice doing this. You have two common options. One option is for you to say, "So, right now, while you sit in front of me, would you get out your own writing and read just the first paragraph as if you are a stranger, asking yourself, 'Does this make sense?' If you spot a place where it is confusing, put a question mark in the margin." The advantage of asking children to try the strategy this way is that you help children apply the minilesson to their own work and help them get started at it. The disadvantage is that, sometimes, kids can't use the teaching point of the day on just any paragraph (as they could in this example), and therefore it is not possible for them to find a place in their current piece where the strategy applies and put the strategy into operation all within just a few short minutes. This portion of a minilesson shouldn't take more than four minutes! Then, too, you can't provide much scaffolding or do much teaching off this work because each child will be working with a different piece of writing.

You might therefore say, "Would you help me with my piece by becoming a reader of my next paragraph? Would Partner 1 read it quietly aloud and, as you read, think, 'Does this make sense?' Partner 2, you listen and give your partner a thumbs up if yes, you think it is making sense." By using your writing for the active engagement, you have a common text to discuss if problems arise in applying the strategy. Also, when children have applied the strategy to your writing, they can transfer the strategy to their own writing once the minilesson is over and they are on their own. Otherwise, the teaching of the minilesson won't carry into the workshop time and may be less likely to carry into each child's writing life.

Sometimes the active engagement portion of the minilesson does not involve partner work; each child works individually, often guided by the teacher's nudges. Teachers listen in on what children do, sometimes intervening to lift the level of a particular child's work. You will often end the time by reporting back on the good work one child did.

The Link

During the link portion of the minilesson, you will usually repeat the teaching point verbatim, adding it to a chart as you do so. You won't have one amalgamated chart that lists every teaching point that has ever been taught! Each chart will feature a collection of strategies writers can use to accomplish a particular goal. That is, the title of the chart generally names the goal, and then below this there will be a growing list of strategies writers might draw upon to accomplish that goal. Charts lose their effectiveness if they are too long. Typically, charts do not contain more than five or six specific items.

Generally, the link is a time for you to tell children when to use what you have taught them. You will be apt to say something like, "When you are [in this situation as a writer] and you want to [achieve this goal], then you might use any one of these strategies," and you reread your charted list. "Another option would be to use this strategy," and you add the new strategy to the list. Usually, in the link, you will say something like, "So today, you have lots of choices. You can do this or that, or this or that."

Plan Conferences, Assessments, and the Rest

Planning a unit can't be equated with just writing minilessons! First of all, once you have planned a sequence of minilessons, you can read through them, imagining the challenges they will pose for your children. You'll be able to ascertain that for some minilessons, many of your children will need extra support, and those will be good places to plan small-group strategy lessons. You may decide that on some of those occasions, you will go from table to table, providing close-in demonstrations of whatever it is you hope children will do first, then circling back for demonstrations of whatever you hope children will do next. For these extra-challenging minilessons, you will probably want to plan follow-up minilessons, devising those after you study the particular ways your children are encountering difficulty.

Then, too, you'll want to plan how you will assess children's progress. You might think that the time to assess is at the end of a unit, but in fact, it is wise to mark several whole-class checkpoints within the unit as well, to tailor your teaching accordingly. One way to do this is to plan to use the checklists and rubrics we have included within this series. You might use them on your own (or with colleagues) after school, sorting students' writing into piles according to where it mostly falls along the learning progressions we've provided. Or you might want to recruit students to join you in assessing their progress—setting them up with their ongoing work and the checklists most appropriate to their development and kind of writing, asking them to see for themselves where they are strong and where they can aim to grow. You might also look back at their work at the beginning of the unit to see what teaching seems to have taken hold since then. In a narrative unit, are they writing about focused events, organizing their narratives chronologically, and storytelling rather than summarizing? In a persuasive unit, are they gathering entries that will help them develop reasons for their opinions? If not, you'll need to plan and devise new sessions accordingly, so you will leave some time and space for sessions you'll create as a result of these assessments.

You can plan for any other aspect of your teaching as well. For example, you could plan how partnerships might be tweaked so that they support the goals of the unit. You might also think about particular language lessons that English language learners may need in a unit.

Because your units of study will be written down, you and your colleagues can put them on the table and think together about these plans. "What's good here that we can add onto?" you can ask. "What's not so good that we can fix?" And that yearly improvement, of course, is the goal for all of our teaching—these units we've crafted as well as the ones you'll invent on your own with your colleagues.